Rob Delaney is an American comedian, actor and writer. He is widely known as the BAFTA-winning co-creator and co-star of the critically acclaimed Channel 4 and Amazon Prime comedy *Catastrophe*, which broadcasts in more than 130 countries.

Also by Rob Delaney:

Rob Delaney: Mother. Wife. Sister. Human. Warrior. Falcon. Yardstick. Turban. Cabbage.

A Heart That Works

Rob Delaney

CORONET

First published in Great Britain in 2022 by Coronet
An imprint of Hodder & Stoughton
An Hachette UK company

This paperback edition published in 2023

1

p. 182: 'Spider and I'
Words and Music by Brian Eno
Copyright © 1999 by E.G. Music Publishers Ltd.
All Rights in the United States and Canada Administered
by Universal Music – MGB Songs
International Copyright Secured. All Rights Reserved.
Reprinted by permission of Hal Leonard LLC

A CIP catalogue record for this title is available from the British Library

Paperback ISBN 9781399710886
eBook ISBN 9781399710862

Typeset in Bembo by Hewer Text UK Ltd, Edinburgh
Printed and bound in Great Britain by Clays Ltd, Elcograf S.p.A.

Hodder & Stoughton policy is to use papers that are natural, renewable
and recyclable products and made from wood grown in sustainable
forests. The logging and manufacturing processes are expected to
conform to the environmental regulations of the country of origin.

Hodder & Stoughton Ltd
Carmelite House
50 Victoria Embankment
London EC4Y 0DZ

www.hodder.co.uk

For Henry's mummy

'A heart that hurts is a heart that works'
– Juliana Hatfield, 'Universal Heart-beat'

'*Pardon this gush of sorrow; these ineffectual words are but a slight tribute to the unexampled worth of Henry, but they soothe my heart, overflowing with the anguish which his remembrance creates. I will proceed with my tale.*'

— Mary Shelley, *Frankenstein*

1

I swim most days now in a pond near our house. There are ponds of various sizes scattered around London, and I'm lucky to live near enough to a couple of them that I can run or cycle a short distance and get wet in a natural body of water. My favourite pond is managed by the city, and if you attend a short briefing, give them eight pounds, and put on an orange swim cap, they let you have at it. It's roughly one mile across and ringed by tower blocks and newer, shinier residential buildings. One time, a heron carrying a dead frog in its mouth flew over me as I swam. I went home and told my four-year-old, and he started crying and told me that the frog was his friend.

Had you told me even five years ago that I would be a habitual swimmer in a body of water that was not the ocean, I wouldn't have believed you. I grew up next to the ocean, at the beach as often as possible, or sailing around the little islands off Marblehead, Massachusetts, in a tiny little sailing boat called a Widgeon. So the ocean was not a problem for me, but I've spent most of my life afraid of lakes and ponds. Frankly, I wasn't even crazy about pools.

The way I intellectualised it was that if something killed me in the ocean, I would understand what had happened; there would be no mystery. My autopsy would read 'shark attack' or 'run down by drunken teenager in a Boston Whaler and hacked apart by engine blades'. It would be awful, but anyone who read the report would understand what had happened. Whereas if I met my end in a lake or pond, that would AT BEST mean that sentient vines had reached up from the pond floor and coiled around my thighs and waist and pulled me down, not even allowing me to scream because they'd tightened around my throat and crushed my larynx. Or, more likely, that the gas-bloated zombie-corpse of a murdered postman had slipped a rusty handcuff around my ankle and was going to yank me down and make me be his wife for eternity.

Better the devil you know – which, in my case, was sharks and drunk teenagers. I suppose I thought dying in the ocean was just the cost of doing business, whereas dying in a lake meant you could only have been murdered by someone or something that derived erotic pleasure from your gurgled screams.

As insane as my aquatic-death belief system was, it was my own and I lived by it for decades. I believed it fervently and planned my swimming – or not-swimming – accordingly. My wife, Leah, however, grew up near plenty of lakes, ponds and rivers, and her mother was her high school's swim-team coach. She'd swim anywhere, anytime. She even went swimming – prepare yourself – in the *winter*. I'd heard about people doing this here and there; like maybe going for an instantaneous dip in Norway if you had a sauna inches from your hole in the ice, or for a similarly brief dunk on New Year's Day in Maine if you had a running car with the heat blasting right at the water's edge. But deliberate, frequent swimming in a natural body of water, in the winter, without a wetsuit, was not something I realised people did. I'd assumed that being in cold water for more than a few seconds meant that you would contract bronchitis or pneumonia straight away, and you should notify your local hospital to have a bed ready, just in case.

We hadn't been in London for too long before Leah had assembled a comprehensive list of local swimming areas, which are myriad, and included lidos cold and warm, ponds, reservoirs and even the Thames, if you're disgusting. I thought, 'Good for her!' I wasn't afraid for her; the bloated postman only wanted me. 'Twas only for me that the slimy vines ran drills, coiling around driftwood and otters, preparing for the day I mustered the courage to enter their murky lair. Others were safe to swim, splash about, 'tube', or whatever else they felt they needed to do.

When our son, Henry, was sick and in the hospital, what Leah needed to do was swim, and many a morning she'd find her way to a nearby body of water for a quick dip. She had friends that did it, and she made more friends by doing it, all of whom seemed like lovely people. Insane, but lovely.

Leah knew about my terror of the deep, but for some reason she didn't think it was worth countenancing in an adult man. So over many, many years she'd invite me to come with her, and I'd conjure a malady whose only remedy was an immediate nap. When Henry was ill, I had far more excuses, but no energy to find the words to use them, so one autumn afternoon, we trundled off to Hampstead Heath, which has a ladies' and a men's pond, and brought our dear Henry and his favourite carer, Angela. Angela stayed with Henry while Leah and I sexually segregated ourselves and walked the short distance to our respective ponds. I took off my clothes in the outdoor changing area and put on my bathing suit. It was cool, maybe ten degrees, but that didn't bother me. I walked purposefully out to the little pier that extended into the pond. It was a beautiful, bucolic scene – to most. But I knew what evil awaited me in the water. I jumped in – and then out, so fast it probably looked like a tape played forward, then instantly backward at the same speed. 'Fuck this,' I thought, as I towelled off. I joined Henry and Angela, and we all waited on the banks of a different pond while Leah swam leisurely, enjoying herself quite thoroughly. I, on the other hand, had narrowly escaped being eaten, or at least aggressively probed, by the amphibious zombie-priest living in a barrel at the bottom of the men's pond. Never again, I vowed.

Some months after Henry died, Leah and I took a scuba-diving course to get certified. Leah had always wanted to do it, so I got us the classes as a Christmas present. The first few lessons were in a leisure centre in Soho. Funny that there are so many thousands of things happening mere feet from you in a city as big as London, and one of them is grieving parents learning to scuba-dive in an old pool on the same street as theatres, pubs and Pret-a-Mangers.

When you learn to scuba-dive, you do all the straightforward things you'd imagine, first studying written material and then learning how all the equipment works and how to communicate with your partner. But you also practise situations for when things go wrong, from running out of oxygen to losing visibility if your mask is compromised for some reason. For that particular drill, we would sit at the bottom of the deep end of the pool with no masks on and our eyes closed for a few minutes, then ascend blindly to safety. Before we submerged, the instructor explained that it would be scary, and we might want to freak out or, indeed, might actually freak out. A couple of people in the class were visibly scared. I was not.

I descended the twelve or so feet and sat on the bottom of the pool in darkness and felt lots of things, but none of them were fear. Mainly, I felt strongly that I was in a situation where, if something went wrong, I could very, very quickly be with Henry. And that felt good. Obviously, there were others around me, and I was being observed by more than one instructor, who presumably had incentives not to let their students die, but when we are under water in blackness, we are some type of alone, whether we're being stared at or not.

I consciously thought, 'I'm quite a bit closer to death twelve feet underwater and without sight than I was a few minutes ago. My son Henry did death and died not long ago. I won't take the regulator out of my mouth and inhale a lungful of water on purpose, but if it got knocked out by another flailing student and my own fin got caught on a drain, and I panicked and inhaled, and they couldn't revive me – well, then that would be okay.' I felt like a lava lamp; the bits of plastic gloop bubbling around in me were actually bits of a dark sort of peace with death, a harmony with the knowledge that my son had died and that my own death would see me walk through a door he had walked through. We would share one more thing together. And that would be fucking great.

When you're a parent and your child gets hurt or sick, not only do you try to help them get better, but you're also animated by the general belief that you *can* help them get better. It might not be the wound-cleaning you personally administer or the medicine you your-self pour into their mouth – you might have to get them to a nurse or a doctor who has the right equip-ment and skill set – but you believe that it's you who will get them to the right place, via car or taxi or, God forbid, ambulance, and that, once there, you'll sit by their side or maybe hold them in your lap and they'll get what they need. Add a little time to mend, heal, rest, and you'll soon have an exciting story to tell.

That's not always the case, though. Sometimes, the nurses and the doctors can't fix what's wrong. Sometimes, children die. Whatever's wrong with your child gets worse and they suffer and then they die. After they die, their body begins to decompose and later it's zipped into a black bag and taken away by an undertaker in a black van. A few days later, your child is buried in a hole in the ground or cremated in a furnace that incinerates their body into ashes, which you take back to your house and put on a shelf. You wish you could take a kitchen knife and stick it into yourself near one of your shoulders and pull it down and across to the hip on the opposite side of your torso. Then you'd tear apart skin, fat, muscle and viscera, and pull your child out of you again and kiss them and hold them and try frantically to fix what you couldn't fix the first time. But that wouldn't work. So you sit there like a decaying disused train station while freight train after freight train overloaded with pain roars through you. Maybe one will derail and explode, destroying the station and killing you, and you can go be with your child. Would that be so bad?

Why do I feel compelled to talk about it, to write about it, to disseminate information designed to make people feel something like what I feel? What my wife feels? What my other sons feel? Done properly, it will hurt them. Why do I want to hurt people? (And I do.) Did my son's death turn me into a monster? That's certainly possible. It doesn't sanctify you. Things get broken. Maybe it's because I write and perform for a living that I can't help but try to share or communicate the biggest, most seismic event that has happened to me. The truth is, despite the death of my son, I still love people. And I genuinely believe, whether it's true or not, that if people felt a fraction of what my family felt and still feels, they would know what this life and this world are really about.

Not infrequently, I find myself wanting to ask people I know and like to imagine a specific child of theirs, dead in their arms. If you have more than one child, it's critical you pick one for this exercise. If you're reading this, and you have a child, do it now. Imagine them, in your arms. Tubes are coming out of various holes, some of which are natural, some of which were made with a scalpel. There's mess coming out of some of the tubes. There are smells. The temperature of your child's body is dropping. No breath, none of the wriggling that seems to be the main activity of kids, no heartbeat. Even just that; imagine searching for your child's heartbeat and you can't find one. Their heart will never beat again. It's not a nightmare you can wake from; defibrillation won't work. It won't beat because your child is dead. After a bit, someone will put them in a refrigerated drawer, like you do with celery that turns white and soft when you forget about it. Did you ever make funny horns on their head with shampoo while they were in the bathtub? You will never do that again. Did they ask for help with their shoelaces and their homework? Did you comfort them after a skinned knee? That will never happen again.

It's unlikely I'll ever ask anyone to do that face to face. Honestly, the idea makes me laugh. Where would we do it? A kitchen, probably. Do I make them tea first? But the point is that I feel the urge. That is one thing grief does to me. It makes me want to make you understand. It makes me want you to understand.

I want you to understand.

But you, statistically, cannot. You forget that my son died. Then you remember. Then you forget again.

I don't forget. I don't hanker for much about Victorian times, but the idea of wearing all black following the death of someone you love makes a lot of sense to me. For a while, anyway, I'd have liked you to know, even from across the street or through a telescope, that I am grieving.

2

I recently found an Excel spreadsheet that I made when Leah was in around her eighth month of pregnancy with Henry. It had the names and phone numbers of people I could possibly call to help with our boys, Eugene and Oscar, when Leah went into labour. We didn't really know anyone in London who we were the type of close with that we could just say, 'Hey, can you watch our boys while Leah has our newest baby?' We didn't have any grandparents or aunts and uncles nearby, nor did we have any long-term friends. We'd only lived in London for seven months at this point, having moved here from Los Angeles in September of 2014 so I could shoot the first series of the sitcom *Catastrophe*.

I suspect most of the acquaintances on the list would've jumped in to help if necessary, but the fact that I made the list at all speaks to the anxiety of living in a new country during a very vulnerable time. I genuinely can't even imagine how awful it must have felt for Leah, even though she will still occasionally tell me. In addition to not really knowing anyone in London as Leah got ready to give birth, we certainly didn't know how London hospitals worked either. So even though this was Leah's third pregnancy, we took the British version of the pre-natal classes we'd taken two babies ago with our eldest, Eugene, back in Santa Monica. The massive difference in this pregnancy was that Leah saw a midwife instead of an obstetrician for her routine visits, which she vastly preferred. All hail NHS midwives and the British method of preparing to welcome a baby into the world. Her midwife visits were even at the nursery (which was also a community centre) that our older boys attended during the week! If you're American and reading this, you deserve to know that she didn't even have to present an insurance card at these visits, or hand over a forty-dollar co-pay. (If you're British and don't know what a co-pay is, remain blissful in your ignorance.) Nor did she receive a bill for it a month later. (She did, however, have to genuflect to busts of Marx and Lenin and hiss at a small American flag.)

We also registered at the birthing centre at the Whittington Hospital, a couple of miles north of our flat. While there are vast differences between British and American healthcare, some things are exactly the same, and one of those is that hospital 'designs' are insane in both countries. This is obviously a result of the fact that they begin as a building that ostensibly makes some sort of architectural sense, but then need to grow as the decades wear on. At that point, they either build a larger building next to the original build-ing, or sometimes put it literally on top of and around the original building. It is CRITICAL that the newer building be wildly different from the original building in design and utility, and it must include things like elevators that can't be accessed without going outdoors and re-entering another part of the hospital, as well as hallways that directly bypass high-traffic wards, allow-ing you to see or hear them, but not access them. Repeat this process every twenty-five years until you have a building that would make Frank Lloyd Wright shake and vomit.

Once I realised that the Whittington Hospital in north London was just as psychotically designed as UCLA Santa Monica Hospital, where our older boys were born, I knew I'd have to do some serious dad recon before I brought a labouring Leah there. So, one Sunday, I gathered up Eugene and Oscar while Leah was resting, and we boarded the bus up to the Whittington. Truly one of my favourite memories as a dad ever: riding on the top of a double-decker to familiarise myself with the route to the hospital, with my trusty lieutenants in tow. At ages four and two, the idea of riding the bus with purpose, to help Mummy, who was getting ready to produce a new sibling for them, was just intoxicating. Their (almost) matching blue coats made them look like official little guys executing a most important task.

We alighted from the bus and explored the hospital's multiple entrances before locating the maternity ward, which was (naturally) way, way the hell back behind a couple of car parks at the back of the hospital. I knew we were in the maternity ward when a nice older woman answered 'Yes' when I explicitly and roboti-cally asked, 'Is this *exactly* where I should take my pregnant wife who is registered at this hospital when she goes into labour soon?' I was glad I had confirmed this, because it was exactly the kind of dark and non-descript entrance that a moron like me could miss with ease. Satisfied that I knew where to take Leah when the new baby decided to join us, the boys and I hit a nearby McDonald's and took the bus back home. I reported back to Leah that I could, with reasonable confidence, get her not just to the correct hospital, but even to its correct entrance, the way a hero might.

Not two years later, Henry would live at this hospital for seven months, after being released from the specialist kids' hospital Great Ormond Street. I would become extremely familiar not only with all the hospital's entrances, but also with all its sprawling grounds, staff car parks, outbuildings where CPR courses were taught to the community, and more. I'm sure I could draw an accurate floorplan from memory.

If I counted correctly, thirteen Whittington nurses attended Henry's memorial after he died.

It's wonderful, and it hurts. I think about him as a little baby, and I think about him as a toddler. I think about the expressions he used to make, and his hands and feet and legs. I think about Henry's hair, every single day. Despite my own full-body coat of fur, Leah and I exclusively produce bald babies. And just as he started to grow hair, they found the tumour in his head and he started chemotherapy. His first hairs fell out and he was bald again, and I would hold his bald head and kiss it and feel the warmth of it. It was such a pleasure to do that. When he grew hair after the chemo was done, we didn't cut it, and, oh my God, it was so beautiful. This long, blond hair, like a gorgeous little bank robber in *Point Break*. I just loved to put my fingers through it and comb it behind his ear and just . . . I get mad when I think about how beautiful he was, and it's offensive to me. His hair, his face, his eyes that were such a bright blue. It makes me angry that people won't get to look at them. Those eyes were two of the most glorious things I've ever seen and it offends me that they're not there for people to gaze into. It's fucked.

In the lead-up to Henry's birth, Leah ordered a portable 'instant' bathtub from Korea. The flat we'd rented hurriedly just before moving to London didn't have a bathtub, and, like pregnant women throughout history, Leah enjoyed a bath while pregnant. At first, she looked on farming supply websites for a feed trough that would fit in our little shower. She scratched that idea when she discovered these waterproof nylon folding bathtubs on the Korean internet that would ship to London. Basically, they're a small fabric 'box' surrounded by a folding metal frame, and one adult can fit in if they scrunch up a bit. If it already sounds fun, get this: the bathtub has a fabric cover you can zip closed, leaving just your head peeking out! How wonderful must Korea be if they can think up something like this? Hats off forever to this wonderful nation. So nearly fully developed baby Henry wriggled around in Leah's womb and Leah wriggled around in a similar level of confinement in her zippy Korean folding bathtub. I smiled every time I saw her, or Eugene and Oscar, bathing in it.

I smiled a lot around Leah anyway. On one of our very first dates, eighteen years ago, we were crossing a street in Santa Monica, and she stopped abruptly before she got to the curb. She then got down on all fours and began to 'climb' up the curb, very slowly and deliberately, as though she were scaling the sheer rock face of a mountain. The sight of an adult woman struggling mightily to conquer a rise of maybe ten centimetres has made me laugh and smile on and off for the last two decades.

Blessedly, my mom visited when Leah was around forty-one weeks pregnant, and we wound up not having to use my emergency spreadsheet to get help with the big boys. After Leah had been in labour for a bit, some of it spent in her little tub, we grabbed her bag and called a taxi to the hospital. Our

ROB DELANEY

neighbourhood is loaded with big speed bumps, and the route to the hospital had maybe 355 of them. Leah's face read 'Are you fucking kidding me?' with each one we hit, and I hoped that each bump would at least maybe subtract a little time from her labour.

We entered the hospital through the door I'd masterfully identified days earlier and headed to the birth centre. As old as the Whittington Hospital was, its birth centre was quite new, and each BIG room had everything you could want to help you squeeze out a critter (as a decorated feminist, I can say with authority that this is how Today's Woman prefers to describe birth). Our room had a birthing pool, a big 'normal' (non-hospital) bed, yoga balls and foam wedges I had previously thought were only for men with ponytails to have sex on with women who use tarot cards to make important life decisions. It honestly would have been a fun hotel room for people who weren't even having a baby. It was wildly different from the extremely 'medical' setting our older boys were born into. Leah had always wanted to do a water birth, but our insurance in the US wouldn't let her. So not long after arriving, they filled up the birthing tub and Leah got in. Her midwife was very, very young, I would guess twenty-five. I recall thinking she couldn't possibly

20

know what she was doing, simply due to the fact that she just couldn't have stacked up enough births yet to be a 'pro'. She had a thick Scottish accent and wore a hijab – an impossibly British collision of attributes that was wonderful. She was, inevitably, a brilliant midwife. Was she better than the old American doctors who had delivered Eugene and Oscar? Yes. Yes, she was.

In the birthing tub, Leah swayed and rocked and breathed her gas and air, while I pretended I'd learned anything from the first two births I'd witnessed. When Henry wriggled out and we saw his little penis and huge testicles, I laughed out loud. A third boy!! A perfect, beautiful boy.

Henry had a wonderful birth. I remember studying his little jaundiced, fuzzy, reptilian body as he was weighed, and marvelling at what a gorgeous creature he was. I was ready to love this boy forever.

A little while later, my mom brought Eugene and Oscar to meet Henry, and we all cuddled in the big bed while Leah and I doted on Henry and his brothers ignored him and gobbled hospital toast with jam as fast as the nurses could bring it to them.

The first year of Henry's life was a tornado. Eugene was four and Oscar was two, so we had three boys under five. I say 'we', but it was mostly Leah, by a long shot. *Catastrophe* got picked up for a second series before the first one even aired, and it didn't occur to me to take a break before beginning work on the second one. We just dived right in, and in my work fever, I let my family simmer unattended on a back burner. Of course, there were moments of beauty and togetherness, and Eugene and Oscar were loving and proud brothers to Henry, who smiled and babbled at them and was just generally a delightful and smooth little nugget we all loved to kiss and squeeze and make laugh.

3

When Henry vomited at his oldest brother's fifth birthday party, we didn't think anything of it; he was our third kid and we'd cleaned up enough gallons of puke not to be fazed. I'd been feeding him blueberries, so there were maybe fifteen or twenty recognisable blueberries in there. Did I question my parenting in letting him eat so many of the blueberries now floating in his puke? Sure. Was I a lazy parent, and had I just let him keep eating them because it kept him quiet? Probably. But I'm pretty sure I let him eat chorizo before he was nine months old. By your third kid, you're not bugging out about every little thing they want to eat. Want some chorizo? Go nuts, little man. Chorizo's good, why wouldn't you want some? I'm glad I gave him the blueberries, the chorizo, and anything else his little heart desired, because not long after his first birthday, he would switch for the rest of his life to a liquid diet that would be delivered through a tube into his stomach. When your kid can only eat PediaSure Peptide through a tube, you'll be happy they ate the chorizo. A few too many blueberries – what's the big deal? Party on.

When Henry vomited two more times the next day, we started worrying and I took him into A&E, to make sure he didn't become dehydrated. The A&E doctor got the idea Henry might have a urinary tract infection, so they wanted a urine sample. Because he wasn't keeping fluids down very well, they asked me to feed him five millilitres of some electrolyte juice through a syringe every five minutes and hold a little cup next to his penis to catch any urine he might produce. Sitting next to him, holding a cup under his adorable little eleven-month-old penis and administering him little squirts of juice every five minutes, was a joy. I couldn't look at my phone or watch *Finding Nemo* on the TV, lest I miss a drop of that precious pee, and we just entered this meditative state, staring at each other. He finally made a little pee and we left with some antibiotics, with the understanding that they'd call us and tell us if a UTI was the culprit. It wasn't.

Over the next couple of weeks, Henry kept vomiting, but not too much, and he seemed to be keeping more down than he was throwing up. We were still concerned, though, so we brought him to our local GP, where he promptly vomited on the floor. I was glad he threw up in front of the doctor. I wanted to point at the vomit on the floor and say, 'See, asshole? That's vomit all right. Now what are you going to do about it?' What he did was give us an appointment to see a gastroenterologist. That made sense to me, since up to that point in my life, vomit-related issues generally centred on the stomach. That doctor gave Henry an anti-emetic, which seemed to work, and told us to monitor him for a while and come back if things got worse.

Then the vomiting plateaued a bit, and we decided to stick to the plans we'd made to visit the United States for the Easter holiday. We missed the beach and our friends, and wanted to visit LA and make sure we still liked it enough to move back there. Our visit revealed that we did indeed, so we began to make plans to return. I'd do one more series of *Catastrophe* and use the money I made as a down payment towards a house in Santa Monica.

We then visited my family in Massachusetts, and while we were there we took Henry to an American hospital. For a 500-dollar deposit, they did an ultrasound on his kidneys to see if they were infected. They didn't seem to be, but they put him on different antibiotics anyway.

Henry's vomiting intensified upon our return to London. We started to get scared. Henry was losing weight and every time he vomited I would freak out, blaming myself for not feeding him gently or slowly enough. Why, if I'd been able to feed Henry's raven-ous, feral older brothers, couldn't I feed him? I started feeding him so carefully it was like I was defusing a bomb. I stared into his eyes for some sign that I'd fed him differently, better, in a way that wouldn't make him vomit. But he would, almost every time. My baby was getting smaller, and that is a fucked-up thing to see. I would imagine collecting the vomit somehow and pouring it back into him with a funnel. His vomit became the most precious substance in the world to me, and I would start crying whenever he threw up. I would try not to cry in front of his older brothers and fail, and they'd ask why, and I would say it was because I was scared.

By this point, we knew we were going to get some kind of bad news; we just prayed it would be coeliac disease or a twist in his gut that could be surgically fixed or something.

Then my friend Peter, whose kids are older than ours, recommended we go see their family paediatrician. In addition to being a kind and thoughtful guy, he was also in his seventies, which meant he'd seen a few more decades' worth of kids and their sometimes-mysterious maladies than your average practising NHS GP. We saw him at his private practice, though like many private doctors in London, he was also registered with the NHS. We were willing to try anything at that point.

Like every other appointment, I took Henry to Dr Anson myself. Leah, who is a magnificent mom and insane about our children, would have happily taken Henry, but for whatever reason I'd taken him to the first appointment, so we just kind of stuck with that and he became my little project. I was on a break between the second and third series of *Catastrophe*, so I had the time. Leah stayed with our older boys, who were five and three and were, frankly, the more difficult job posting.

Dr Anson called Henry and me into his office. He was pleasant and avuncular. He checked out Henry and was as alarmed as anyone to see the loose skin on his inner thighs.

He asked some routine questions, but then he asked one that stood out from the others: 'Is his vomiting effortless?'

'Effortless?'

'Yes. Does he retch, or seem distressed when he vomits? Or does it just come up and out?'

'Hmm, huh, um. It is effortless, yeah. He's not troubled at all.'

'Okay, I think we should schedule an MRI. Of his head.'

'Okay, why?'

'Just to make sure there's nothing in there that shouldn't be. Pressing on his emetic centre, making him vomit.'

'What, like a tumour?'

He paused. 'I'm glad you said it.'

That conversation, understandably, is seared in my mind. And yet so many of the days, months and years that followed are obscured by a fog. Grief drove a bus through the part of my brain where memories are stored. I forgot the PIN for my ATM card. I'd been using it for years, and it just evaporated from my head. I had to get the bank to send me a reminder in the mail.

Some time after Henry died, I got a call from a guy who was helping me write jokes for an awards show I was hosting. We'd been working closely together for a couple of weeks, and he called to review some stuff and said, 'Hey, Rob, it's Mark.'

'. . . Mark.'

'Yeah, Mark?'

I felt like I was being asked to find an individual lentil in a warehouse that a tornado had just blown through.

'Mark, apologies, but I do not know who you are.'

'We've been working on your speech for the awards show next week?'

'Oh, Christ, that's right. I'm sorry. Mark, the fact is that grief has fucked my memory. Don't take it personally; what's just happened here is not an isolated incident. Sorry.'

It felt weird to say stuff like that to a guy I didn't know well, but it didn't feel as dishonest as not saying it. I could let the Marks of the world think I was going senile early, or I could tell them the truth, which was that the pain I was in, missing my little boy, had wreaked havoc on me mentally as well as emotionally.

*　　*　　*

When I left Dr Anson, I was stunned and terrified and called Leah. She was with her friend, Australian Leah. Australian Leah had a daughter called Bea who was a few days younger than Henry, and the two of them liked to lie near each other on the floor and wiggle. Later on, Bea would come and visit, and she didn't really seem to notice that Henry was quite disabled and Henry didn't act like anything other than the mayor of the whole ward. They were an adorable pair. When I see Bea these days, it is unbearably painful, and I stare at her and wonder what she and Henry would get up to if he was around.

Henry and I got in a taxi to see Leah. We cried and hugged and marvelled together at this horrible news. Australian Leah cared for us. Our gorgeous boy, who'd been losing weight and getting smaller and weaker and disappearing in front of us, might in fact have a killer inside his sweet little head.

Dr Anson had told us that Henry needed an MRI to confirm it was a tumour. I would, of course, become very familiar, in the months and years to come, with the sickening anxiety of waiting for scans and their results, but this was our first time enduring that terrible pillar of the cancer experience.

On the day of the MRI, we took him to the hospital and they put him in an adorable little gown with red, green and yellow cars and trucks on it. For the first of so many, many times in his short life, sweet Henry was anaesthetised. We cried and tried to smile for him and make him feel safe. We kissed him, and then we were ushered out of the room.

Dr Anson told us that the MRI would take a while, and that once Henry went in, we should probably go across the street to a little Greek café and get a bite to eat if we were up for it. After pacing up and down corridors for a bit, Leah and I made it across the street to the café and ordered some food. We held hands, thrumming in fear, fully cut off from our bright, bustling surroundings. As the waiter delivered our order a few short minutes later, Dr Anson ran in dramatically, the tail of his coat flapping behind him, and he told us to come back to the hospital immediately. We abandoned our baklava, I threw money on the table, and we raced out after him.

In his office, Dr Anson confirmed that Henry had a large brain tumour in the back of his head, near his brain stem. He delivered the news calmly, and ended by saying a paediatric brain surgeon would come to see us within a few hours. We sank inside ourselves.

The heaviest pain in the world. I felt like I had suddenly quadrupled in weight, and an oily, black whirlpool began to swirl where my heart had been.

Dr Anson said we could go and see Henry, so we left his office and headed down a flight or two of stairs. Along a corridor, Leah found an unoccupied breast-feeding room and went inside and started screaming. I held her.

When we were able, we left that room and walked out of the building and across the street to the one Henry was in. We were led to Henry, who was just waking up, and Leah tenderly picked him up and hugged him and kissed him. I wrapped myself around Leah and Henry. He looked at us, tired and confused. He had turned one less than two weeks before.

One. One. A one-year-old boy. I had consciously looked forward to Henry turning one because I had so enjoyed the other boys when they were one. One is such an amazing age. Most one-year-olds can do almost everything an adult can, except use a toilet and talk. AND they haven't yet started the phase of toddler-hood where they're wilful or even a little bit naughty. They're genuinely very fun and interesting, but they're still wildly needy and will allow you to cuddle them and kiss them literally all day if you need to. Nothing but nothing is more joyous than a one-year-old.

Leah used to make me laugh when Eugene was one by saying happily to him, 'You've never done anything wrong!' He would walk out of our front door in Santa Monica in nothing but a nappy and then just head off down the sidewalk exploring, dragging a free advertising circular he'd found behind him. I would stay close, but just follow him and watch him encounter birds and cats and interesting parked cars. We had wonderful mornings where Leah would stay in bed, pregnant at the time with Oscar, and we'd just wander happily. Discovery is a one-year-old's entire MO.

When Oscar was born and one-year-old Eugene met him in the hospital, he walked up to Leah's hospital bed and kissed Oscar's feet.

Then when Oscar turned one, I was so excited because I had some idea of what to expect. It was the same, and it was so different, and I realised that each child is their own unique engine of discovery. At some point, Oscar realised I seemed to read more to Eugene, who was now three. He waddled to a pile of books, picked a couple up, then waddled back to me, gently pushed me down on the floor and got on top of me.

Jesus, that made me happy, a little one-year-old chunker knowing what he wanted and then going and getting it.

So, as Henry's first birthday had approached, I'd occasionally think, 'Oh boy! Here comes one!' However, even before he started vomiting and losing weight and we struggled to get a diagnosis, Henry had seemed younger than the other boys at his age. I would often say to Leah that he seemed like our 'babiest baby'. He didn't crawl and 'cruise' as manically as our other boys did; he didn't seem eager to walk. He was less energetic. I figured it was simply that different kids develop at different speeds; he'd do his discovering on his own terms.

It was excruciating to learn that the real reason was something other than his brain was taking up a lot of space inside his skull.

Of course, there's no fourteen-month period you'd want to spend in the hospital, but given the option, I bet to fuck nobody would pick your second year of life, when you're exploding developmentally and growing and learning so much. I hated that he spent that time in surgery, recovery, physical therapy and chemo, calling a hospital home while his peers were learning to walk and babble and play around on splash pads at the park. Because of his beautiful brothers, I knew well what he was missing, and it made me fucking angry and sad.

Sitting with Henry in those hours after his MRI, after we found out about the tumour, we weren't thinking about the next year of his life; we could only think about the next few days. Eventually, a brain surgeon from Great Ormond Street Hospital came to the private hospital and introduced himself to us. He was a nice, calm, quiet guy named Mr Elsawi. He said we were going to get to know each other well, which was both comforting and upsetting. He told us that Henry had a tumour the size of an apple near his brain stem. (How the fuck do you fit an apple in a kid's head? I guess you don't. It makes them very sick and then it kills them if you don't get it out.) He told us he would open Henry's head in a few days and try to remove the tumour. We digested that news, and a little while later, Henry and Leah and I were taken to Great Ormond Street Hospital. It was interesting to experience something I'd heard before, which is that if an MRI (or any test) finds something truly and dangerously wrong with you in a private hospital, you'll often be put in an ambulance and sent to an NHS hospital.

Great Ormond Street Hospital is one of the leading children's hospitals in the world. They don't have a maternity ward or an A&E; it's a specialist hospital for kids with specific and serious illnesses and conditions. If your kid is very ill in the UK, it's where you want them to be. It was a beautiful Friday evening in April. There was a glorious sunset visible between the tall buildings of north London. We passed couples on dates and people smiling and drinking pints outside pubs as we were driven in an ambulance to what would become Henry's new home.

Upon our arrival, Henry was admitted and given a bed in their brain and neurology ward.

We were shown to a shower room where all three of us could fit in, and Leah showered with Henry, holding him. I took their picture and in it, beautiful naked Leah is cradling beautiful naked Henry under the warm water and the expression on his face is one of pain and fatigue you would normally associate with an old man.

In those first few hours at Great Ormond Street Hospital, we met doctors and nurses who'd seen Henry's type of tumour before. They were calm, purposeful. We were disorientated, and in shock. Hours after his admission, they decided they had to do an emergency surgery to relieve pressure on Henry's brain so he didn't haemorrhage or have a stroke. It was a Friday, and his big surgery was scheduled for Tuesday, but the pressure was so severe it couldn't wait until then. (This would begin the trend of Henry having almost every emergency on the Friday leading into a bank holiday weekend, when doctors and nurses, just like normal people, like to go to the beach or maybe a wedding in Canada.)

While we waited for that, Henry ate the last food he'd ever eat. It was a chocolate croissant from the hospital cafeteria.

They took him and did a four-hour surgery to put a shunt in his head to relieve the pressure on his brain. He came back from surgery with his lovely little head all wrapped in a white gauze turban. He was tired and weak and woozy. We held him and loved him and got ready for the big surgery a few days later.

Leah's parents, Nancy and Richard, and my mom flew in to help before the surgery. My younger sister Maggie wasn't able to fly over from Boston right away, as she was a primary school teacher, plus the grandmother who would have babysat her two-year-old daughter Marie was now in London, helping me.

Maggie was 'best maid' at my wedding, and we'd been very close since she was born, five years after me. Probably due to the healthy age gap and the fact that we were different genders, we always got along very well.

My mom likes to tell people how, if anyone ever gave Maggie a treat when she was little, she would always say, 'And one for Robby.'

Maggie was married to a wonderful man named Tobias, for whom she'd fallen pretty hard several years earlier. My whole family fell for him, to be honest. He was a kind, gregarious, intelligent guy, who really fulfilled a 'solar' social role in that he warmed everybody up and people were happy to rotate around him and bask. He also had a couple of degrees from Harvard, but we didn't hold that against him.

In those early days, I spoke to Maggie and Tobias on the phone regularly and they offered comfort from afar. And we couldn't have got by without our parents there, helping with the boys, cooking meals and holding our hands. They were shellshocked too, but they'd showed up and that's what mattered.

One day, Leah and I were both home at the same time with the big boys, Leah's parents and my mom. We were all shaken and red-eyed. At one point, I started crying, and Leah came over to comfort me. Then Richard put his arms around both of us and said, through his own tears, 'I wish it was me instead of Henry.'

'We do too, Richard,' I said, and everyone laughed.

4

As he'd predicted, we got to know Mr Elsawi, Henry's surgeon, pretty well.[*] I smiled when I learned that he rode a motorcycle to and from work every day: operating on brains, all day, every day, and then riding the vehicle that multiplies the likelihood you yourself will need brain surgery by 800 per cent. Naturally, we learned a lot about brain tumours in the months that followed. For example, brain tumours are now the leading cancer killer of children. It used to be leukaemia,

---

[*] I am calling Henry's surgeon Mr Elsawi instead of Dr Elsawi due to the fact that in the UK, male surgeons are addressed as 'mister', to distinguish a surgeon from a physician. This tradition dates back to the 1800s when medical licensure in the UK was a mess and almost any asshole could go and get an 'MD', either from abroad or a questionable school in the UK. So the surgeon's 'mister' is different from my 'mister' and is certainly different from a mere 'doctor', and in a UK hospital setting everyone knows it. I like all the weird historical medical anachronisms as it reminds me that as genuinely miraculous as surgery and medicine are, there remains an element of 'Hey, man, let's open 'em up and see what's going on in there,' just like there was 300 years ago and beyond.

but since leukaemia was (and, of course, still is for many) so deadly for so long, it got a lot of attention and research, and they were able to help more and more kids survive it. Not yet the case with brain tumours. Also, paediatric cancer is much rarer than adult cancer. Thus, it's less lucrative for drug companies to work on therapies that help kids. To any toddlers reading: yes, capitalism solidly and demonstrably places your grand-father's recovery from cancer above yours.

Mr Elsawi explained that the tumour was right next to Henry's brain stem and probably wrapped around important cranial nerves. He hoped he'd be able to get it all out because it was probably malignant and of the sort where you couldn't leave any of it behind, or it would grow again. He said if he couldn't get it all out in one surgery, they'd have to do another.

We spent the four days leading up to Henry's big surgery in terrified anticipation. The surgery would take all day, so Leah and I got a hotel room close to the hospital. We settled in, and in an effort to dull our senses we watched some *Big Bang Theory*, *How I Met Your Mother* and *Friends*. No *Seinfeld*, though. Brits are psychotic about *Friends*, but *Seinfeld* didn't hit as big over here, which doesn't reflect well on them as a nation at all.

At the hotel, we were so crazy and scared and hold-ing each other so tight, we actually wound up having sex, twice, a few hours apart. I realise it sounds insane to say that we had sex twice while our one-year-old had brain surgery across the street. I would normally omit that very personal fact, which might horrify some people, but I am sharing it primarily for the benefit of other parents who might have been through something similar and were terrified and crying and nearly hyperventilating with anxiety. I guess we were just so scared and wanted to be so close, and the horror of what was happening around the block didn't erase the fact that we loved each other, and sometimes that love manifests as sex, even in the absolute worst of times. It's probably good that we did, because in the months to come, the fear and anxiety would not always be kind to either of our libidos.

We were able to check in with the hospital and knew that everything was progressing in a fairly normal fashion. After about nine hours, we were losing our minds, so we went back to the hospital and milled around a parents' lounge in a trance, occasionally lying on the floor. After thirteen hours, we were told the surgery was done and we could see our beautiful baby boy. This surgery was, of course, much, much more devastating to his body than the one a few days earlier, so he was immobile in a bed, hooked up to numerous machines. A brutal sight to see. We kissed him and told him we loved him.

Mr Elsawi said that he had removed all the tumour he could find. They'd opened Henry's head via an incision in the shape of a big '7' on the bottom back of his skull. Then they'd taken a piece of skull out and done their best to get the tumour out. It was fine work, first debulking the large tumour and then scraping remaining bits off the brain stem and cranial nerves. Mr Elsawi said the tumour was hard and dense and had been growing for a long time; Henry may even have been born with it. 'Their best' was pretty good, as subsequent MRIs would not show any tumour.

Henry had a vast number of tubes and wires attached to him and going in and out of orifices, and cannulas going into various veins. He also had burns all over the front of his torso. The pad they had him lying on during the surgery was the tiniest bit too hot, so over the course of the thirteen-hour surgery, it had cooked the beautiful, smooth, delicate skin of his tummy and chest. The burns healed quickly as they weren't that bad, but right after the surgery, he was covered in these red welts. Apparently, burns from heating pads during surgery aren't wildly rare, but it was unsettling to see his gorgeous skin damaged over such a large area. It speaks to how surreal and horrifying the situation was that a square foot or so of burns on our one-year-old's body was maybe the eighth-worst thing we had to deal with in the early days after his surgery.

Now our concern was his recovery from the necessarily brutal surgery on his brain stem. The brain stem controls many of our involuntary processes, like heartbeat and breathing, and is also part of what's often called our 'lizard brain', as it's among the first parts of the brain to have developed evolutionarily over the millennia, well before the more mammalian parts that enjoy Chekhov and fantasy football. When you fuck with the brain stem, the recovery process is steep and long. We had no idea how brutal it would be.

In the months and years that followed, both Leah and I wrestled with guilt and would allow ourselves to wonder if the stress of our move to London with her pregnant and caring for a one- and a three-year-old, plus my working too much, had somehow created a fertile environment for a tumour while Henry grew inside Leah.

I think it's understandable that we wondered that, but then of course many (most?) pregnancies are stressful, or even take place in literal warzones, and a perfectly healthy baby is usually the result. Similarly, we all know of someone who never smoked and got lung cancer. I am sceptical of those who claim to know the reason one person got cancer and another didn't – unless it's one of those very obvious cases, like your drinking water came from a reservoir next to a factory being investigated by Erin Brockovich.

Some people should feel guilty, though. Early in our hospital stay, I got a call from the publicist at my management company. He told me that the *Daily Mail* had called and were aware that I had a son in Great Ormond Street Hospital being treated for a brain tumour, and wanted to know if I wished to comment. I told him to please tell the *Daily Mail* that if they printed anything about my son, I would kill the reporter and any editors who approved it, and then sit down in a puddle of their blood and wait for the police to come. No article ran.

A few days after Henry's surgery, we were allowed to carefully hold him on a pillow. He'd have to be gingerly lifted out of his bed by two or three people, making sure none of his lines and ventilation got tangled, but we could hold our baby boy again. The weight of him in my arms was heaven. The ability to kiss him, to put my lips on his tummy and his shoulders. His ears weren't yet freed from the bandages, but I would get to kiss and nibble gently on those soon, too. He was quite knocked out from the surgery. He did start to wiggle about and respond definitively to all our stimuli, however, and was very awake and alert after a week. Things like crawling or cruising, however, were gone for a long time, and would need to be relearned.

The big motherfucker, though, was that he had lost the ability to swallow. They told us he might regain it in time. They did two tests to determine the damage to the cranial nerves that controlled his swallow. One test involved a neurologist hooking up some electrodes to his head, neck and face. He said some version of 'Not looking good,' and then they did test two, which consisted of removing his breathing tube. Henry began to struggle pretty quickly and I began to cry, and I'm crying now typing this. He couldn't breathe and he couldn't prevent saliva from going into his lungs. It was horrible, and I prayed he would cough and gasp and all his muscles and nerves would get shocked into working again. They didn't. After I don't know how long, they put his breathing tube back down his throat, which was also a brutal procedure, and after calming down somehow, he began to get the oxygen he needed in an unimpeded manner.

To manage his breathing and swallowing, Henry got a tracheostomy – a breathing tube inserted in the base of his neck – and we became experts in its care. That's discussed enough elsewhere in the book, so I'll just say I hated that fucking thing and I also wish to hell I was still spending a good portion of each day doing his tracheostomy care. If you ever see a kid with a tracheostomy, you are looking at a bad motherfucker, and I can also promise you that their parents would be of genuine use in a field hospital.

Throughout the torture of removing the breathing tube, its reinsertion, and the recovery from the tracheostomy itself, Henry did not cry. That's because a common effect of surgery on your brain stem is that you lose the ability to cry for a few weeks or months, as crying is one of the earlier things humans learned to do, and is thus controlled by that oldest part of the brain, which, in Henry's case, was totally fucked up. So we cried for him.

*   *   *

I dream about Henry often. I dream he's alive, and in those dreams it's not as though he was never sick. He's the Henry that might have survived, some possible future where he still needed help with a few things. So in my dreams, I'm still caring for him. We do things together; I even take him with me to work. In some dreams, he's recovered, and sometimes his cranial nerves have been repaired somehow, and it all works out. He runs into his mother's arms. He plays with his brothers, or even fights with them, and I love it all.

Other times, I'll dream about a terribly wounded animal that I'm frantically trying to fix, but I don't have the proper tools. I wake myself up crying and struggling to breathe. I love these dreams. They hurt like hell and terrify me and make me feel close to him.

In the days following Henry's surgery, Leah and I moved into housing next to the hospital that is provided for parents whose kids are in the paediatric ICU, or 'PICU'. It was not unlike a college dorm room, and I really can't overstate how wonderful it is that the hospital provides this service, given you're not allowed to sleep overnight in the ward. You can kiss your child goodnight, then go across the street and sleep in an actual bed, then get up and go see them first thing in the morning. For whatever reason, the place we stayed was called the Italian House, a name that is reminiscent of films where James Bond or Ethan Hunt would hide at some spartan safe house while waiting for instructions, impatiently watching for an envelope to be slid under a door with some passports and cash, or details of the next target. What we'd do, however, was sit and digest each day's events, processing and coordinating all the information we'd received, trying to make sense of it and figure out what questions to ask the next day

In the early days, I would stagger between the Italian House and the ICU and invariably pass lots of kids in the hallways. Because I was spending so much time in the paediatric intensive care unit with mostly inert kids hooked up to machines, the sight of ambulatory kids talking and smiling and using their limbs with wild success just absolutely blew my mind. I wanted to grab them and manipulate their arms and legs like marionettes. I wanted to thrill them and terrify their parents by yelling at them, 'THOU ART AS A GOD ON EARTH. I BATHE IN YOUR PERFECTION!' Instead, I'd stagger back to the Italian House and stare at the ceiling, my head on fire.

Our bed in the Italian House was a plastic mattress that got very hot as our bodies cooked off the day's stress, but we did have a bathtub, and our windows looked out over a courtyard that appeared to belong to a nursery. It was decidedly carceral, but it also gave me and Leah time to process and bond. We both look back on it as a tender, painful, yet special time. We were in hell and we were loving each other.

We would soon become acutely aware of how lucky we were to have two heads to put together to navigate all the necessary medical decisions. I don a clownish variety of hats and take each off, one by one, out of respect to single parents who deal with similar challenges. We were also absurdly fortunate to happen to live not far from Great Ormond Street Hospital, whose rooms held kids from all over the country and, in some cases, the world. Countless kids were there with one parent, while the other parent was back in Stoke-on-Trent or wherever else with their other kids. It was clear to us that, as bad as it was, it could have been worse.

5

Not long after his tracheostomy, Henry got a serious infection. After the brain stem is disturbed through surgery, an infection a normal kid could fight off easily can become deadly. Additionally, breathing through a new hole in your throat also opens the door to more – and worse – infections. Henry was very sick, and it looked bad. The nurses and doctors began to act with greater purpose and solemnity. There seemed to be more of them around his bed. His room *felt* bad.

Lunchtime rolled around one day and Leah and I decided to walk a couple of blocks to a Lebanese restaurant for some falafel. Normally we'd get take-away, but we sat down in the restaurant to talk. We agreed it seemed like Henry might be preparing to die. Neither of us had wanted to acknowledge that in front of him. We sat with that. We didn't come up with a plan or anything; we just sort of accepted that it was by no means a foregone conclusion that we were in a tunnel from which we would one day emerge into light. We also breathed in the reality that it was very likely that something other than the cancer itself would kill Henry.

But the infection didn't kill Henry. He eventually responded to antibiotics and improved over the course of a week. He smiled when his brothers visited, and we all kissed him and squeezed his little feet.

It often felt like we were falling down a flight of stairs in slow motion with each successive piece of bad news we got. First there had been a mystery illness, then the mystery was 'solved' when we found out it was cancer. Then the surgery to remove the tumour disabled him terribly. Then the subsequent surgeries to address the damage to his cranial nerves left him susceptible to fatal infection. One day, we were going through the notes on his surgery and learned that the nerve that allowed him to hear with his left ear had been severed, and the nerve that went to his right ear was damaged. Discovering weeks into hospital life that, on top of everything else, he was deaf in one ear and hard of hearing in the other was emblematic of the whole vicious experience; a terrible, knock-on development with massive conse-quences that was buried among everything else to the point where we'd almost missed it. He tried a hearing aid for a while, but it relied on an elastic band that went around his head and irritated the shunt that drained excess cranial fluid into his stomach. So after he took it off in frustration for the fiftieth time, we didn't put it back on again, and just favoured his right ear when we spoke to him.

After two months in the ICU, Henry moved into one of Great Ormond Street Hospital's several cancer wards. Most diseases and conditions have only one ward – one for renal diseases, one for respiratory conditions – but cancer needs a few, since it's the big killer. Henry's oncology ward was called 'Giraffe'.*

Just before moving the few floors to the new ward, we went to a weekly meeting of parents of the kids

* If I ever needed to reach the ward on the telephone for some reason, I would first call the main hospital switchboard, where a robot would try to route your call. It would say, 'Please state the name of the ward you're trying to reach.' The first time I called, I said, 'Gi-RAFF,' in my American accent, to which the robot said, 'I'm sorry; I didn't understand. Please state the name of the ward you are trying to reach.' I yelled 'Gi-i-RAAFFFF' a few times, with increasing frustration. After no luck, I wondered if the robot wanted me to say 'Gi-RAHFFE' in an English accent. I tried it and was immediately connected to the ward. The point is, you never know the battles people fight in secret, and I am a victim of racism.

who were receiving treatment and living there. It was awful. One mother dominated the meeting, complaining about the hospital's food. That wouldn't affect us, since Henry didn't eat food. The other main theme of the meeting was how to properly clean the microwave in the parents' kitchen to protect the kids whose immune systems were weakened by chemo. Again, Henry didn't eat. I'm sure those groups were helpful for some, but at the time it just made us feel even more isolated. We never went back.

Henry had what's called a grade-3 ependymoma, and chemo is not always part of the protocol for that type of tumour. Ideally, they'd have liked to do proton-beam radiotherapy, but in another nightmare aspect to the whole thing, doctors really don't like to give radiotherapy to kids' brains if they're under three, as even the most focused radiotherapy generally guarantees some level of permanent brain damage. The decisions you have to make are all fascinatingly terrible. One thing that helped us decide what to do was the fact that Henry was too fragile to go home anytime soon. So we figured that since he'd be in the hospital anyway, we might as well begin chemo.

We were told his pee and poop would be poison to us, so we should wear gloves when we changed his diapers. I never did. Maybe because he was our third, and by then I could change a nappy reasonably well enough not to get too much on me? I also didn't want to put on fucking gloves to change my son's nappy. It's an intimate act of care for your kid and he had enough gloved hands touching him. I'd wash them afterwards, anyway.

Henry had Bell's palsy on one side of his face because of nerve damage, so half of his beautiful face was slack, which was beyond charming-looking. It makes an already chubby toddler cheek even chubbier. He was such a beautiful, fucked-up boy. These gorgeous little imperfections compel you to be very careful; you know you're handling something precious: the Bell's palsy, the surgical scars on his head, his little bald head when his hair fell out from chemo. And his 'Hickman line' – the permanent port through which chemo was administered, which went through a vein in his chest and then into a larger vein near his heart. My favourite thing to do was to press my eye socket against the roundness of the back of his soft head and feel its warmth radiate into my eye. A fuzzy chemo head is unique in its softness, with its wispy almost-hair. It was so wonderful, I couldn't keep my head and my face and my lips and my eyes away from it. I held his head and kissed it and absorbed its warmth through my eyes.

In the paediatric oncology ward, we met the nurses who would come to define our relationship with the NHS. The PICU nurses were great, but it was so intense there, it's hard to remember names and faces. But in Giraffe, Henry began to fall in love with nurses – and so did we. He was in Giraffe getting chemo for several months, going through cycles of treatment and recovery that left him by turns sick, exhausted, and desperate to play games like any other one-year-old.

Henry's favourite person at Great Ormond Street Hospital was an HCA named Katie. HCA stands for healthcare assistant, and while they're not nurses (though many are students on the path to a nursing degree), you don't need a degree to dole out TLC. Katie, being caring and smart and formally en route to nursehood, was often assigned to care for Henry throughout the day. She quickly became very good at tracheostomy care, and while she couldn't administer chemotherapy, she could certainly attend to its side effects, maintain a safe airway for Henry, and most importantly, read him stories and sing songs and play with him. Katie was but one of the many wonderful NHS workers who took brilliant care of Henry, but it says a lot that the NHS employee who burns brightest in our memories was among the youngest (twenty-three!) and among the lowest on the totem pole, as HCA is an entry-level position. She just had an enthusiasm for looking after 'the whole kid', meaning that while all the medical i's and t's were certainly dotted and crossed, she gave equal attention to making sure Henry had a smile on (half) his face. I DON'T KNOW how many times I walked into his room to find them singing and signing 'Incy Wincy Spider', or playing in a little plastic bathtub on the floor, or hunting for little dinosaurs in a huge bowl of dried lentils.

And Katie was not unique in this aspect, as gifted as she was. Many other staff nurses and senior staff nurses did the same wonderful things. Katie happens to be the one that Henry forged the first and deepest connection with, so that's why I'm shouting about her here. There are many Katies within the NHS. One major source of anxiety for me in writing this book is that I cannot name and celebrate everyone who made substantial contributions to the quality of Henry's life, and our lives.

One thing I will say is that the NHS is such a glorious institution that I almost can't believe it exists.

Discovering it in my late thirties was a revelation. I remember going to the local GP soon after we'd moved to London to register our family. I entered nervously, as walking into a medical facility when you're American usually means you're about to part with money, or at least learn about ways in which you will be parting with money if you actually dare to use any of its services. I was asked for our address and dates of birth, and I provided them. 'What else do you need?' I asked, feeling my wallet pulse in my back pocket.

'That's it,' they said.

'Right!' I remembered. 'I'm in the UK!' We were here on a valid visa, we had paid the healthcare surcharge the Cameron–Clegg coalition had intro-duced in 2015, thus we were allowed to use the NHS to our hearts' content. And use it we did. It was just staggering to go to the doctor and not pay anything out of pocket, since taxes covered it.

A discussion of national healthcare policy would be a book unto itself, but I would be remiss if I didn't flamboyantly function as a sort of 'Ghost of Christmas Future' for my British friends due to my (and every American's) experience of the for-profit healthcare nightmare. The growing number of politicians and newspaper-owners who aim to privatise the NHS need to fuck off ten times, then gargle a big bowl of diarrhoea. I pray that Vishnu purifies your heart in a dream tonight, or, failing that, that you fall down a deep well in February.

The biggest smile I've ever seen in my life was when a little therapy dog visited the paediatric cancer ward at Great Ormond Street Hospital and came into Henry's room to play with him.

I don't really like tiny dogs. I can get to know and respect individual small dogs, but as a concept, they generally bum me out. I guess it's because I know human beings had a hand in their breeding and I believe that to be wrong. Let dogs fuck each other (or not, if you spay/neuter them), and stay out of the way. Don't decide which dogs should fuck each other so that you can wind up with a litter of miserable, shivering little abominations that will fit in a cereal bowl when fully grown. Plus, do you watch the dogs fuck each other and/or assist them? Psychos. Do you punish them if they refuse? Anyway, it's clear my issue is with the dog-breeders themselves more than their cursed progeny, but I can't help but be reminded of their origin when I hear some yappy little shitbox barking at the heavens, knowing deep inside that God has forgotten about it.

The dog who visited Henry was wonderful, however, and it forced me to confront deeply held prejudices, a practice I usually try to avoid. Well into his chemo treatment, Henry was weary, bored, and wanted to go home. One morning, a very sweet woman came to the door of his room and asked if he'd like to meet Lola, a little brown-and-white dog who liked kids. 'YES PLEASE,' I said and they came into the room.

I detached whatever tubes or feeds I could, and picked Henry up and sat him on my lap on the floor. I wanted to make sure he felt safe and was comfortable with the dog. He instantaneously wriggled out of my lap and onto the floor so he and Lola could kiss and hug. HE WAS SO HAPPY. The paralysis on the left side of his face meant the intensity of the smile on the right side of his face was just off the charts. Your smile and my smile are more or less symmetrical, but since only half of Henry's face could smile, you could actually measure just how wildly different his happy-to-kiss-and-be-kissed-by-Lola face was from his resting expression. When I look at pictures of the occasion, it almost looks like he's straining his face; like the amount of sheer joy was slightly too much for a human face to safely express. It was easily, easily the most beautiful smile I have ever seen in my life. His little nappied bum sitting on the linoleum hospital floor, his legs splayed out with his little orthopaedic black shoes, his smooth, chemo-fuzzy head, and the purest expression of joy you could imagine. Thank you, sweet Lola and Lola's friend, a wonderful volunteer who brought her in on her free time to meet kids dying of cancer.

If you happen to be reading this book because someone you love is sick, or you yourself are sick and in the hospital, I really can't stress enough how important it is to do things like play with a dog while you're getting treatment. Holding a dog (even a small one) and letting it lick your face is absolutely just as important as your chemo, your radiation or any surgery. Why? Because it fucking works, right then and there. Will your chemo work? Maybe. Radiation? Perhaps. Will holding a little Lola and playing with her make you smile your face off? Yes, it will, right then and there. Don't need a prescription, and you don't need to sign a disclaimer before you do it. Do dogs have germs? Maybe? Probably? I don't care. I recall the doctors and nurses saying that a lot of the infections and illnesses that occur during the immuno-compromising that comes from chemo arise from germs and bacteria we carry in and on our bodies all the time anyway. So, you're going to get sick from your chemo either way; why not get sick having fun? I remember asking Henry's lead oncologist if it was okay for us to take him to a local park somewhat early in his chemo treatment. He said something along the lines of, 'You better take him to a park!'

To which we said, 'But isn't his immune system quite weak?'

'Indeed it is, but he'll enjoy the park and that's very important.'

Great Ormond Street Hospital took incredible care of Henry, and we adored his nurses and healthcare assistants and play therapists. He thrived, in his way, and was often happy. He also became an accomplished pickpocket. Due to his magnetism, nurses loved to hold him and play with him on his mat on the floor, and just generally be close to him, and often when they left him they'd discover he'd stolen their pens from their shirt pockets. He'd (half) beam with a big smile when they returned to get whatever he'd taken.

Due to the warmth of the care he received, Leah and I made the decision to start sleeping at our home. This decision was difficult but not excruciating, since, as I've mentioned, we lived pretty close to the hospital. We decided to do this for a couple of reasons. One was that due to Henry's complicated tracheostomy, a nurse or healthcare assistant spent the whole night in his room. The other was that Oscar and Eugene were three and five, and they needed us too.

6

People often asked me if writing the fourth series of *Catastrophe* was therapeutic, since it came so soon after Henry's death. I don't know the answer to that. I think art is an incredible, wonderful, healthy place to process feelings of all kinds, but I am also inclined to think that I go to therapy for therapy, and wouldn't want to put any kind of hope, pressure or requirement on my work to 'heal' me, as much as I enjoy it. At the same time, I put a lot of pain into *Catastrophe*'s scripts and performances. We wrote the third series when Henry was ill, and the fourth after he died.

For a good while after series three of *Catastrophe* came out, I didn't even know if we'd do a fourth. Channel 4 in the UK and Amazon in the US both wanted more episodes, but making the third season had been very difficult. Henry was in the hospital while we wrote and shot it, and I really didn't like not being with him all day every day. Thank God that

Leah had told me that she would divorce me if I made a third season the same way we'd made the first two. I hadn't known there was more than one way to make TV – especially if you're writing it, producing it and starring in it. I thought, perhaps understandably, that you had to devote every waking second of your day and night to it. I was a total workaholic and a very shitty husband during the first two seasons of *Catastrophe*. Leah had taken a leave of absence from her teaching job (the one that paid the bulk of our bills for years) and agreed to come to London for six months while I tried to make a TV show. And she did so with our three-year-old and our one-year-old, AND she was pregnant with Henry! And? We didn't know anyone in London! And we moved to London in autumn, the season that is right before winter, when the sun sets criminally early in the afternoon. Did I make sure to move us into a basement flat where the view *up* out of our bedroom window was rubbish bins? You bet I did. Did I spend fourteen hours a day working? Routinely!

I really, really don't like seeing this written down. I was a bad husband and a very, very good cog in the TV machine. To explain, I can only offer that I recognised this was my shot, at age thirty-seven, to solidly 'break into the biz', and I falsely assumed that to do so, I should or could hit 'pause' on my family responsibilities. I'd like to invite any and all readers to slap themselves at this point, on my behalf, to underline with a physical sensation that one cannot hit pause on family responsibilities. It cannot be done without inflicting genuine damage. And genuine damage I did inflict! All while pretending to play a loving, attentive partner and dad on a TV show that would be advertised on buses that would drive by and splash my wife, who'd be pushing a double buggy *while pregnant* to go buy nappies and toilet paper for me and my children to use as part of our respective shitting processes. I luxuriate in shame.

Blessedly, the embers of self-respect within Leah did not go out, but sprung into orange flame, and she told me to get my shit together quickly or she would leave me. As part of our arrangement, I would significantly reduce the number of hours I spent writing with my writing partner in the show, Sharon Horgan, and we would get an assistant. Days after agreeing to those terms, Sharon and I won the BAFTA for comedy writing. The very day after that, a doctor told us Henry might have a brain tumour, and scheduled the MRI that would confirm it. I reduced the hours I spent writing on the show even more, and as a result learned a wildly valuable lesson about working in a much better and more focused manner. And our scripts improved!

One thing I loved about writing seasons three and four of *Catastrophe* is that we rented offices to be near Henry's hospital, and then after he died, my house. These were weird office spaces where nobody in the surrounding offices was involved in entertainment, and that gave the proceedings a showbiz-less feel where we weren't tempted to do anything but work. There's a writing tip for you! Get an office in a boring neighbourhood where it is impossible that Maya Rudolph or Frankie Boyle will be working next door and constantly come barging in because they forgot their wallet or want to run a bit by you.

Leah and I met in 2004 when we were volunteering as counsellors at a place called Camp Jabberwocky. Camp Jabberwocky is on Martha's Vineyard, just off the coast of Massachusetts. It was founded in the 1950s by an English speech pathologist (and mom and widow) called Helen Lamb, as a camp where people with disabilities could enjoy summers with a full range of wild outdoor activities. As it's difficult physical work to help people with certain disabilities windsurf or do a ropes course, the camper-to-counsellor ratio is 1:1. Thus, during our first weeks of getting to know each other, Leah and I were also helping our respective campers (both of whom had cerebral palsy) to swim, act in a full-scale musical, or use the toilet. I fell harder and faster for Leah than any woman I'd ever met before, and I told her so a few times a day.

A year later, we got engaged, and a year to the day after that, we got married on the top of a mountain in western North Carolina. We are now more than half-way through our second decade of marriage. I am enjoying the second decade more than the first, because I have learned, through suffering, that my relationship with my spouse requires just as much attention as my relationship with my kids. FEEL FREE to judge what I'm about to share, but I honestly thought in the earlier years of our marriage that I could sort of dip in and out attention-wise, as it suited me, because Leah was a self-sufficient adult. Sure, I loved her and even liked her, but if I didn't want to talk to her about a particular thing or sound her out emotionally before I made a big decision, that was fine, because she wasn't a child who depended on me for food, shoes, etc. That approach really didn't work and if I hadn't corrected my course, it would have led to divorce. You only coast downhill . . .

I can only ascribe my getting a handle on things to grace. Grace visited me and explained to me that my relationship with my wife was not one that I could take for granted – if I wanted it to last. Well, grace and the thunderbolt of Henry's illness.

We made an active decision to protect our marriage, day in, day out, throughout Henry's illness. The way this manifested was simple. Leah and I would go on a date once a week, even when Henry was in the ICU. Didn't have to be a fancy restaurant with a tablecloth. It could be a walk around a park, holding hands. It could be breakfast near the hospital. But we had to look at each other and touch each other and check in and see how the other one was doing. Then we carried that communication through the rest of the day, touching, speaking, just listening to each other's voices. And in the evenings, if we weren't so shattered we fell asleep in front of the TV, we would read aloud to each other. Leah says that reading to each other is so wonderful because it's both active and passive. You're lying there being entertained, even if you're the one reading, and you're using your imagination much more than if you're watching TV. And then you can discuss what you've both been imagining. Our longest-serving companion during this time was Michel Faber's 900-page saga *The Crimson Petal and the White*. It's a luxurious saga set in 1870s London, and it transported us quite thoroughly to a different world, for which we were grateful. Unfortunately, in that world a major character also died of a brain tumour.

I hesitate to give advice, but I have to say that if you're ever in a situation like the one in which my family found ourselves, do not forget to love, touch, and look into the eyes of every other family member regularly. Early during our time in hospital, I started to think of us as five fingers of the same hand. Every finger is important, even the crooked and/or hairy ones. There is a temptation to only pay attention to the patient, especially if they're a young child, but you ignore other family members at your peril. I can't speak for my Henry, but I'm willing to bet he was happy that Leah and I took good care of the brothers he loved so much, and each other.

Henry's brothers were so wonderful with him. Eugene was five when Henry was diagnosed and six when he died. Oscar was three when Henry was diagnosed and four when he died. They were such a beautiful little clump of boys. They loved him so much and he loved them back. For most of the first year of Henry's life, I would sometimes consciously think, 'How lucky are we to have THREE healthy kids? All three of them are healthy. Not every kid in the world is healthy, but these three are. We are so fortunate.' Yes, I really thought that. Probably said it to Leah, too. Parents have countless ways to marvel at their offspring and that was one of mine.

Eugene and Oscar were twenty-two months apart. Oscar and Henry were twenty-five months apart. So they were just a little team of dudes. I remember hoping when Eugene was born that he'd be a girl. I thought for some reason that a daughter would awaken my paternal feelings more strongly or something. Nonsense. I was insane about him from the second he ski-balled out of his mother's vagina. Then when Oscar came out and was a boy, I was actually a little upset for maybe eleven seconds. I guess I thought we 'deserved' a girl to round things out. But then Oscar, covered in amniotic goo, spoke to me and informed me that I'd love him forever and melt anytime he walked into a room. I immediately obeyed – and I still melt when I see his beautiful smile. When Henry came out and was A THIRD BOY, I just laughed. Of course he was!

I'll say here that we never found out what sex our kids were before they were born. Thank Christ Leah and I both agreed on that. Despite the popularity of finding out beforehand these days, the practice still boggles my mind. WHAT the fuck are you going to do with that information? Practise wiping yellow, liquidy shit off an anatomically correct doll? Enjoy the mystery for a few months!

We had our almost-year of relative health with the three boys, not knowing that a tumour was growing steadily next to Henry's brain stem. Once the nightmare of his diagnosis and surgery and disability and chemo and all that entailed became our norm, we did our best to be a family that was spread over two hospitals and our home. The 'big' boys came regularly to the hospital. It is endlessly hilarious to me that we called (and still call) Eugene and Oscar 'the big boys' when they were three and five and charged with helping their parents deal with the mind- and body-numbing responsibilities of caring for a one-year-old with brain cancer. And I can tell you they did an amazing job. Since we were in paediatric wards in both hospitals, there were play areas with indoor and outdoor sections and genuinely fun toys, books and art supplies. The big boys would play there and bring Henry to these areas when he was able to go. They would also happily and obediently sit on his hospital-room floor, eating cookies and practising signing with Henry, Leah and me.

We did every holiday in Henry's hospital room too. Halloween, birthdays, Christmas. And guess what? We usually enjoyed them. We have one Halloween picture where we're all dressed as skeletons. And if you can't have fun dressed as a family of skeletons in a paediatric cancer ward, I don't know what to tell you.

7

One evening, Eugene, Oscar and I were at Great
Ormond Street Hospital with Henry. We'd had
McDonald's and played with him. Read some books
and watched some cartoons. Leah came in and relieved
us, as she was going to spend the night in his room to
observe the night nurses and practise some of the skills
she'd need when he was finally able to move back
home. She'd come in with her lovely friend Clare,
who'd wanted to see Henry and be with Leah, as she
did throughout those months.*

* Advice to people who have a friend or relative with a very sick kid:
get right up their ass and go spend time with them. They'll kick you
out if they need to, but don't waste their time by saying, 'If there's
anything I can do, just let me know.' That's for you, not for them. You
might as well yawn in their face while looking at something more
exciting over their shoulder. Go feed them, visit their kid, touch their
kid, hold their kid, and usher them out the door to take a walk. 'If
there's anything I can do . . .' Yes, you may clip my toenails and clean
my kitchen while I'm asleep. Why are you waiting? You asked if there
was anything you could do. Clare was one of those people who didn't
ask; she just showed up.

I caught Leah up on the afternoon's events and we hugged and kissed goodbye. I took the big boys and we left the hospital, said goodbye to the nurses, and went to get the bus back to our flat a couple of miles away. Double-decker buses had in no way lost their novelty for us, so we climbed the stairs to the upper level. We squeezed into the front two seats and watched London from on high out the window. My phone rang and it was my sister, somehow sounding dreamy and focused at the same time.

She told me that Tobias had jumped off a bridge over a highway just outside Boston and was dead.

I don't know what I said to her. I think I walked away from the boys so they wouldn't hear what we were talking about. I became conscious that the bus wasn't moving and hadn't moved in a while. I'm sorry I don't remember what I said. Words of love, probably, since that's how I usually talk to her anyway. A commitment to come see her immediately and help? Maybe that's what I said, as it's what I would soon do. The bus wouldn't move. There was construction work near a big junction. I took the boys down the stairs and off the bus, and we walked past the construction site and looked for a taxi. They didn't know their uncle Jojo was dead. They loved him and he loved them. He was a very good uncle, a fun, kind, attentive uncle. They were going to be so sad and confused. They ran in front of me down the street and my mind violently recoiled at the thought of telling them.

In the taxi, I called Leah and told her quietly. She started to sob loudly. She loved Tobias so much. He was intelligent and curious and loved to talk big ideas, just like her. The nurses suggested she go home, and when she arrived we sat together, stunned. Our one-year-old son was getting chemo after a brain surgery that had disabled him, and now our beautiful brother-in-law lay in a morgue. Everything hurt.

How do I speak about Tobias? Until a few months earlier, I hadn't even known that he'd been grappling with depression. I guess I felt that my own struggle with depression and the fact that I took medication – and had been quite open about it – meant that I might somehow receive priority alerts if someone anywhere in my orbit was similarly afflicted. That wasn't the case, though.

You don't have to fall in love with your sister's husband. I know plenty of people who haven't. But I so sincerely looked forward to seeing Tobias on every visit home. As did Leah! Leah and Tobias were THOROUGHLY happy to hang out together. They could roll their eyes at any of the odd characteristic behaviours that develop in any family over the decades. They didn't merely 'love' or tolerate each other, they liked each other. We all liked each other.

Months before, my sister had told me that Tobias had become increasingly depressed over the previous year, until he shocked everyone by checking into the hospital one day, afraid for his sanity. At the time, their daughter Marie was two years old, and they'd been speaking about having more kids. Maggie thought they were planning their future, the family they'd have.

Under normal circumstances, I would've been way more involved and up in Tobias's shit trying to figure out what I could do to help. But tiny one-year-old Henry was hooked up to machines at Great Ormond Street Hospital in London, so that commanded just about all of my waking thoughts. I also figured that since Tobias had had the courage to seek help for his depression, it would probably all work out, even if they had to fiddle with his meds for a while to figure out what worked for him. I'd had a couple of terrifying episodes not long after I'd got sober, many years ago, and had come out the other side with the help of medication and therapy. After a week or so in the hospital, Tobias checked out, was on meds and, crucially, many people who were close to him knew he was wrestling with something very serious. I guess I thought that the honesty and sunlight he'd chosen to let in would take care of it.

I'd visited Tobias and Maggie a few months before he died, not long after he came out of hospital. He and I went for a drive together on a warm, beautiful day and I gave him my spiel, which probably included my basic beliefs that depression is brutal and viciously hard, and that it's A-okay to find it terrifying. One of the worst parts of depression is that in its cunning, it wholesale convinces you that it will last forever. But that, of course, would be impossible. That is, I suppose, what I'd say to anyone dealing with it. I said it to him: it won't last forever because it can't last forever because NOTHING lasts forever, even (and perhaps especially) feelings you WISH would last forever. That was one of the most massively helpful things I learned in my early years in AA. Another is that even if you don't believe something, you can kind of lean on other people's beliefs when you're really down. Do you believe that *I* believe it? That type of thing. Do you think I'm an asshole idiot? Do you think you're an all-knowing cosmic despot? Why don't you just leave open the possibility that others love you, whether you like it or not, and that the people who'd like you to stick around aren't, to a man, wrong.

Those are the types of games I played with myself when I was dealing with some very strong suicidal ideation, during the two horrific episodes of depression I dealt with. Episodes that got me on the medication I take to this day.

We were driving around Gloucester, Massachusetts. I'm not sure we were even going anywhere specific. I just wanted to get Tobias out of the house, talk to him. He seemed pretty fucking down and I felt a barrier between us. After half an hour or so, we drove home and didn't speak about anything serious for the rest of my trip. That was in the summertime, a short trip with the older boys to try and provide a little normality for them. Then, in the autumn, Tobias checked himself into a facility again. I see that as such a massive act of courage and love for his family. A fucking SECOND self-admission to a hospital for depression in a year? How brutally difficult that must have been. Of course, I kept in regular touch with my sister, and she detailed how scary and difficult it was. But I didn't fly back and take him and hug him and hold him and wrangle his doctors and make them hammer out a one-week plan and a three-month plan and a six-month plan, and I didn't move into his house and try to muscle him into mental health, which I perhaps would have done had Henry not been in the hospital. I'm sure some of that urge comes from the fact that there was nothing we could do that would've kept Henry alive, so I wanted to believe there was some plan of action that could've kept Tobias alive. I don't know.

I flew to Boston for Tobias's funeral. My mom and I held Maggie as she vomited into the gutter before getting into the limousine to go to her husband's funeral. Tobias looked so handsome in his coffin. He looked beautiful.

After the funeral, I flew back to London and took a taxi from Heathrow directly to the hospital, where I went into a surgical theatre to hold Henry down while they repaired his broken feeding tube.

A month or so after Tobias died, my mom and sister decided to get grief tattoos. To get inked up, they went to a shop in Salem, Massachusetts, a town most famous for murdering witches in the seventeenth century and then selling spooky T-shirts celebrating that fact in the twentieth and twenty-first. After getting their tattoos, they went across the street to a bar to have a glass of wine. While seated at a table, a man they knew walked up and said hello. My mom asked how he was and the man said, 'Ugh, terrible. Really going through a lot. My daughter got married a few months ago, and now she's getting divorced. It's so awful.'

'Oh no, that's too bad,' my mom and/or sister said.

'How are you, Maggie?' said the man.

'Pretty bad. My husband died by suicide a month ago. We have a two-year-old daughter. I don't know what to do.'

The man was dumbstruck, as this was clearly many thousands of leagues beyond his coping skills. He blinked a couple of times and looked at my mom. 'How's Rob? I hear he's doing really well in London.'

My mom's eyes sparkled and she looked at Maggie. 'Should I tell him?'

'Go ahead,' said Maggie.

'Well, Rob's one-year-old son is in the hospital getting chemo for a brain tumour. He was disabled by the surgery to remove the tumour, so Rob and his wife are having to learn a lot of difficult medical stuff to help him. He's had some close calls with infections. They're having trouble managing three young kids between the hospital and home. So he's not doing great.'

At that point, the man essentially shut off mentally and staggered away. Maggie and my mom started laughing hysterically. The cackling, dolphin-like laughter of the insane that surely would have seen them executed by the state had it occurred on the same spot 300 years earlier.

And we are insane. Or it's as though we live on some lunar outpost. I benefit profoundly from the fact that my sister lives there too, but at the same time, I wish her life had unfolded in a way that let her live somewhere else.

Tobias died in October 2016 and Henry died in January 2018. So, in a fairly short period of time, tragedy left us both prostrate on the same floor. Maggie and I don't have other siblings, and we have always been very close. As the dominoes fell, we were as shocked as we were devastated. Here's the order: Henry is diagnosed with cancer and disabled by the surgery to remove his tumour. Tobias seeks inpatient help twice, a few months apart. Tobias dies. Henry's cancer returns and we learn he'll die. Henry dies.

What? How? It would have perhaps made sense if they'd died in the same fire or car accident, but every time it enters my consciousness that they died in such temporal proximity to each other, it is just mind-boggling to me, and I have to tell myself that yes, that's what happened.

In between their deaths, I read Joan Didion's *The Year of Magical Thinking*. In the beginning of the book, when Didion's husband John Gregory Dunne died, I was mostly unaffected emotionally. Dunne was seventy-one, and I was hoping my two-year-old would make it to three. Seventy-one felt like a good run. Dunne died, however, while his and Didion's daughter, Quintana, was unconscious in the hospital with pneumonia and septic shock. As Didion settles in to ride these twin waves of horror, I started to buzz. I didn't (couldn't) respond to a senior citizen dying, but once the widow he's left behind has to tend to her unconscious daughter in an ICU while freshly grieving her life companion – well, that was the book I needed at the time. I've been sober for twenty years, but the sensation that book gave me was analogous to three beers and a bong hit. Didion made me feel less alone.

I called Maggie and told her about it. We laughed at the fact that reading about someone being dragged by the ankles through hell could just absolutely wash me in the waters of peace. Didion herself would die not quite four years after Henry, in December 2021. So long, Joan, and thanks for the laughs!

The support that Maggie and I have given each other over the last few years would be difficult to explain to anyone else. Checking in with her is critical for me, and the same for her. I wish fate hadn't given each of us the exact necessary qualifications to genuinely and substantively help each other, but it did, and we use them. What a fascinating cunt of cosmic symmetry. When one of us cries to the other, we don't try to fix it; we don't stammer platitudes. We just listen and hold.

8

Henry spent seven months at Great Ormond Street Hospital. After that, he no longer required their specialised level of care, so he moved on to the Whittington Hospital, where he'd been born not quite two years before. We resisted the move to the Whittington at first, as the only place we wanted to move him was home. Plus, I was filming the third season of *Catastrophe*, so Leah had to do the move herself. We were also told the Whittington didn't have anyone trained to care for his type of tracheostomy.

Of course, the Whittington and their staff proved to be wonderful. They quickly got up to speed on his trache and his other complex medical issues. More importantly, they engaged with him as a child with desires and thoughts beyond the physical. One ward sister would let him sit at the front desk with her and greet people as they entered the ward, his half-smile beaming out at them. He had great physical and play therapy there, and he loved their indoor and outdoor play areas, which were well stocked with toys and a little 'kitchen' he could work in. He and Oscar would ride tandem on the various scooters and trains.

While living at the Whittington, Henry would be shuttled back to Great Ormond Street every two weeks to get chemo. It made him sick, which would have to be managed so that no infections got out of control. With each successive dose, he'd get a bit sicker. Finally, one day around six months in, we were at the Whittington and Henry got very sick, very quickly. The nurses and doctors recognised it as sepsis and sent us in an ambulance to Great Ormond Street. We rode in ambulances frequently, but this was the only time the driver blew through traffic, blue lights flashing. The nurse riding with us was crying because Henry was so sick.

When we got to Great Ormond Street, a decision was quickly made to remove Henry's Hickman line (the permanent port through which they delivered chemo), which they identified as the source of the infection. Once we settled on that game plan, Leah dashed off to run Eugene's sixth birthday party at the local leisure centre, and I stayed with Henry. That's division of labour when you have multiple kids and one has cancer. As I sat waiting for Henry to leave surgery, I realised it was exactly one year since Henry had first vomited at Eugene's fifth birthday party.

After a few days of treatment, Henry recovered from the sepsis, but the infection signalled the end of his chemo course. Unlike a course of antibiotics, which you need to complete in order for it to work, chemo, while it involves unbelievably powerful drugs that are very carefully dosed and administered, has an element of 'Uh . . . let's just see what the patient can handle' to it all. The doctor knows the drugs will make the patient sick, and they have to recalibrate and adjust as things progress. Henry had had a great deal of chemo and its side effects (a weakened immune system that made him susceptible to sepsis) were becoming untenable; we decided he'd had enough. Plus it was just awful to watch him improve after recovering from a dose of chemo only to see him knocked back down by the next dose. It physically pained me to sign the consent forms each time he got chemo. Speaking of brains, my own frontal lobe knew chemo could 'help' him, but my brain stem knew even more deeply the pain I was consigning him to.

It was thrilling to know Henry wouldn't receive any more chemo. While I'm fully aware that chemo cures cancer in many cases, it's also easy to imagine a time in the not-too-distant future when our grandchildren will say, 'You fucking did WHAT to people with cancer?' Doctors describe it as a blunt tool for a reason.

A couple of years after Henry died, I noticed it had been warm and sunny for a few days in a row. What was that about? The calendar said it was April. Spring? I realised that I hadn't registered the change of seasons for a couple of years. It had been such a slog taking care of Henry at the hospital and his brothers at home, while trying to make sure everyone could be together as much as possible, that I just hadn't been aware of my surroundings on a larger level. Obviously, I must have been cognisant on some level of the number of layers I should put on myself and the boys when we went outdoors, but beyond that I didn't really observe, record, or react with any joy or wistfulness as seasons passed. It was nice to feel the warmth and hear the birds, but the fact that I was allowing myself to do so was because Henry was dead.

In all the months Henry was ill, normal stimuli hadn't operated on me in the way they had before.

Details and information from the larger world that would previously have affected me exercised limited to no influence on the fact that my son was dying and then dead.

Throughout his illness, we were entertaining the idea that Henry could live. We couldn't really imagine a future where he wasn't disabled to some degree, but we thought (and were told) that it was possible the cancer wouldn't return and he may one day not require a tracheostomy. We greeted the MRIs that happened every three months with roiling terror and anxiety, but they continued to be clear.

And we were together, watching Henry grow and change. Even as he was receiving chemo and other treatment, Henry was changing into more and more of a little boy rather than a baby, working out who he was, fleshing out his role in the family.

Henry had a funny pair of green glasses that had sort of plastic 'blinds' that ran across where lenses would have been. He loved to take them off Leah and put them on me, then do the reverse. He was an avid drummer and liked to play the triangle. Like any toddler, he loved bubbles. He loved to 'shoot' his brothers with a wand and make them fall down, via dark magic. He loved to dance too, particularly to the song 'Sexual' by the artist NEIKED ft. Dyo. Leah would hold him and they would BOOGIE.

During this time, while he was still receiving chemo, Henry began physical therapy, and I am immediately, right this second, smiling thinking about his PT sessions. The hardest I have ever seen anyone work at anything was Henry doing his physical therapy. The women who handled his PT were all so wonderful. They would give him his little exercises, such as 'high kneeling' (lifting his bum off his feet to a kneeling position and holding himself there), and then they'd gently coach him through it. He did so well and worked so hard. To witness a one-year-old, receiving brain chemo, work so hard with such profound limitations was just beyond astonishing. We'd watch him cruise around on a walking frame called the 'Rifton Pacer', a name that always made us laugh ('Be right back, I'm Rifton Pacing!'). His drive to live and to learn and to grow is the most powerful force I've ever seen. If you think you've praised your child for a job well done, I wish you could have seen Leah or me go absolutely bananas in support of Henry picking up a cup from the floor and placing it on a low table, while kneeling. Einstein and Serena Williams can fuck off; Henry was a true achiever. Oh, oh, how we loved to help him with his exercises and kiss him and hug him when he'd finished them.

Reflecting on his physical therapy reminds me that I'm not a fan of the 'fighting' metaphor for cancer. I don't think you fight it, or beat it. The effort I saw Henry expend, again and again, at the age of one, under such duress, suggests someone who could beat anything that *can* be beaten. Cancer's pretty much going to do what it wants. Should it come for me, I hope I'll just ride the wave.

It should surprise no one that after Henry was diagnosed and began his new life in the hospital, I began to listen to a lot of Elliott Smith. I'd always loved Elliott Smith, but now that I had a child in mortal danger, whose life would at the very least be dramatically transformed forever, Elliott Smith felt like the right soundtrack. For anyone who doesn't know, Elliott Smith was a genius whose music was already considered depressed – and, to some, depressing – even while he was alive. But then in 2003, he died after stabbing himself twice in the heart with a kitchen knife, really cementing his legacy as the immortal Prince of Sadness or whatever. It's 'funny' that a couple of years before that, Wes Anderson actually filmed Luke Wilson's character slitting his own wrists in *The Royal Tenenbaums* while Smith's 'Needle in the Hay' played in the background.

Even more remarkable than all that was the fact that in 2002, while Smith was still alive and working on his final album, I was in a sober-living halfway house with an extraordinarily prescient Elliott Smith superfan. His name was Greg, and like some in the house, he had just got out of prison. I hadn't been in prison myself; just the rehab that would mark the beginning of the now twenty years I've somehow been sober. Greg was a big, muscly Italian kid who could've benched me and Elliott Smith at the same time, but he loved to sit with a guitar and sing Smith's songs beautifully. Greg had a new, bumpy, ugly red scar in the shape of a big 'T' on the left side of his neck. Why? A few months earlier, he'd tried to kill himself by – you guessed it – plunging a kitchen knife into his own neck. I don't know what became of Greg after the few months we lived together in the halfway house. All these years later, I just remember that I liked to hear him sing and play the guitar – and that he owes me thirty dollars, which in today's money is closer to forty-seven dollars. Greg, if you're reading this, keep the money. Just don't spend it on knives, you nut!

If that's not enough, another housemate from sober living was a very handsome and skinny junkie who used to play with Elliott Smith. He said that part of his motivation for going to rehab was spending time with Smith, whom he viewed, even while alive, as a cautionary tale.

So, that's the type of music I wanted to listen to every day when Henry was in the hospital. Now, granted, I'm a sober alcoholic who's taken two antidepressant drugs every morning for most of the last twenty years, but for me, Smith's music isn't depressing at all. Even after years of managing depression with reasonable success, I don't pretend to fully understand why I feel that way about his music, nor do I opine on it that much. I can say that I love and take comfort from things that others might casually dismiss as depressing. Am I giving myself homemade exposure therapy? I don't know. Maybe it's like how I now love it when people bring up Henry. If they worry, I assure them they're not really 'bringing him up' at all; I was probably already thinking about him anyway. Similarly, Smith's music and other music that might seem – or even be – sad or blue makes sense to me, because I listen to it and think, 'That's how I feel inside,' so why not accept that and listen to music that helps me find some equilibrium between my interior and my exterior?

One signature of Elliott Smith's music is that he often double-tracked his vocals so it sounds like there are 'two' of him singing on most of his songs. He didn't harmonise; there are just two of him, almost like a quiet echo that's simultaneous. It's a beautiful, ghostly effect you might not immediately put your finger on, but you notice after a while. Sometimes, I like to imagine that there were two Elliotts, and the one who couldn't handle this world did indeed leave us, but the other one quit the music business and is off somewhere, fat and happy.

Before I quit using Spotify because they (with the encouragement and assistance of record companies) fuck artists out of so much money, I used to enjoy getting my end-of-the-year wrap-up that tells you what hundred or so songs you listened to most that year. Horrifically enough, in 2016 EVERY SINGLE SONG BUT THREE were by Elliott Smith. Good thing my therapist doesn't get alerts from Spotify, because he would have had a SWAT team extract me from wherever I was and take me to the nearest residential psychiatric facility. The reddest of flags! 'His "Spotify Wrapped" was all Elliott Smith?? Who saw him last?? Can we get a visual?? Go! Go! Go!'

The three songs that weren't Elliott Smith were by an Icelandic artist named Ásgeir. I think I first heard him on BBC Radio 6. Ásgeir has a couple of albums that are absolutely in league with Beck's *Morning Phase* in terms of mellow beauty and gorgeous complexity.

I would listen to Ásgeir's album *Dýrð í Dauðaþögn* while Henry napped in his hospital bed. As complex and wonderful as the album is, it's also calm enough that a one-year-old can nap through it. So, Henry and I listened to it many, many times when his afternoon nap rolled around. I'd get him comfy in his bed and then I'd lie down on the little bed they had for us to rest in next to him. We'd listen to Ásgeir and drift off and dream together. What I would fucking give to do that again. To sleep next to and dream with my beautiful boy. If I died tomorrow, those would probably be the greatest memories of my life. A boy and his daddy together, dreaming and sleeping. Sleeping and dreaming. A machine occasionally beeping. Nurses in the hallway. Maybe I'd get up here and there to suction his tracheostomy. But mostly dreaming and sleeping. Sleeping and dreaming.

Two years after Henry died, Ásgeir released a new album. I cried and cried listening to it, wanting so badly to share it with Henry.

Some months after that, I was directed by an Icelandic woman in a television show and I told her that I loved Ásgeir. She said she did too, and she asked me if I knew about his father. I said I didn't. She told me that Ásgeir's father was a poet, and that he wrote all of Ásgeir's lyrics. I was stunned. The music Henry and I listened to together most, in an almost holy setting, was also a collaboration between a son and a father?

Glorious.

Unbelievable.

9

Henry's tracheostomy tube prevented him from speaking, so by his second birthday, we hadn't heard him make a peep for nearly a year and we knew we might never again.

Most of the time, he had a foam-cuffed tracheostomy tube in his beautiful throat, the care of which took up a considerable amount of time and energy. The hole in his throat was about the same circumference as a bullet hole, and it needed about as much attention as a bullet hole does.

I got to know his tracheostomy nurse very well. She had been a colonel in the British Territorial Army, and had served in Iraq and Afghanistan. She also helped turn Great Ormond Street Hospital for Children into a triage unit for adults on the day of the 7 July 2005 bombings in London that killed fifty-two people. I must also mention that she had a crush on the actor

Mark Harmon, and brought him up in conversation more than once. No judgement; I bring up Alicia Keys out of the blue now and then, and that's okay. This nurse taught me to care for the hole in my beautiful baby boy's neck, in a way that was as vital as it was agonising for him. I fucking hate that I had to do it at all, but I'm grateful to her for teaching me, and for talking me back to sanity afterward.

After he lost his voice, Henry communicated through Makaton, a language programme that uses symbols, signs and speech to enable people to communicate who might otherwise have a tough time being understood. Many people with Down syndrome find it helpful, as do kids like Henry who can't speak due to a tracheostomy and nerve damage. You may have seen Makaton if you've ever watched the beloved Mr Tumble on CBeebies. Mr Tumble is the alter ego of a guy named Justin Fletcher. Since he's probably the most famous Makaton user in the UK, he's helped countless families develop communication skills that foster substantively better and closer relationships. It is fair to say that I love him. One time I heard a mom talking about her preferred CBeebies shows and she said she didn't like

Mr Tumble. I had to walk away. Fuck with Mr Tumble, and you fuck with me! She's lucky I had errands to do and didn't have time to go to jail that day.

I've yet to meet Mr Tumble, but I have had the good fortune to meet Singing Hands, who probably brought Henry the most joy out of anything in his sweet little life. Singing Hands are Suzanne and Tracy, two wonderful women who (among MANY other things) have their own channel on Great Ormond Street Hospital's televisions. They perform all sorts of songs and nursery rhymes using Makaton and their lovely singing voices. The second we found their channel, Henry was hooked. A channel made for kids just like him! We watched Suzanne and Tracy sing each song again and again, and Henry and Leah and I practised signing along. It was so goddamn fun. And Henry was GREAT at it. His tumour and surgery only affected his physical skills, but had had no noticeable effect on his brain's frontal lobe. So he was as alert and curious and driven as any other kid.

One day, I was down in the Great Ormond Street cafeteria (getting a Bovril, maybe?) and did a double-take. Tracy from Singing Hands was there, sitting at a table, just like a normal civilian might! I took a deep breath and approached her with the mix of purpose and humble deference with which a normal person might approach Sir Paul McCartney. I told her I was one of, I'm sure, thousands of parents whose ability to communicate with their child was directly improved by her beautiful work. She didn't ask me to please back away from her table, but rather was happy to hear about Henry, and about how her and Suzanne's work had affected us. She even asked if she could come up to Henry's room and meet him. And meet him she did. Henry was agog. He was confused at first, like anyone would be if one of the coolest people in existence essentially walked out of the television, but kids adapt fast, so he soon achieved equilibrium and seemed to think, 'Yeah, this tracks; she must have wanted to meet me. Exciting women dig me.' Months of incessant, doting attention from all the nurses had done its work. He was so happy to sign 'Incy Wincy Spider' and 'Mary Had a Little Lamb' and other nursery rhymes with her. So was I! Tracy and I kept in touch, and in time we would meet Suzanne, too.

A little less than a year after Henry died, I was asked to read the CBeebies Bedtime Story. If you're not British, the BBC has a channel for little kids called CBeebies, which probably does at least 25 per cent of the UK's parenting. It does it well, too. Its programming is excellent – high-quality and educational. Shows like *Something Special*, *Hey Duggee* and *Bluey* entertain kids (and adults) with wildly creative, sensitive, stimulating shows – and they're not interrupted by commercials. And at the end of each programming day, at 6.50 p.m., a different celebrity reads a story before they turn out the lights. I'd always wanted to do one and was thrilled to be asked. I asked if I could do my story in Makaton.

CBeebies were happy to oblige, and I was surprised to learn that I'd be the first ever Makaton Bedtime Story. We'd agreed that Penny Dale's version of *Ten in the Bed* would be a good book to do in Makaton. I practised in the days leading up to the recording, and on the appointed day, I went to the London hotel in which we'd record. They had me on the edge of a bed with the ten necessary stuffed animals perched across it. They also provided a lovely Makaton coach, who made sure I did all the signs perfectly. The recording went reasonably well until I had to sign and say the phrase, 'I'm cold and lonely.' I started to cry. It just shook me to know that I'd be doing a book that Henry loved, using the method of communication I'd eagerly learned for him, and he wasn't alive to see it. Of course, I was desperate to get it on TV so other families could watch it and use it, but it hurt terribly to do something he'd have enjoyed so much. The producer said we could take a break if I wanted to, and I said no, I am crying because I miss my son Henry. I learned Makaton for him and now he's dead. So I am going to take a few deep breaths and we can continue filming.

I didn't mean that to chastise a lovely person for humanely and very understandably offering me a break; I just knew that disabled kids and their families deserved their first Makaton Bedtime Story, and it was our job to get it on the air. It was one of those instances where I felt the show, as it were, must go on.

It did, and when that Bedtime Story went out, people really loved it. Seeing the happiness it brought kids and parents who need Makaton to communicate flooded me with love and gratitude for my sweet, blessed Henry. His death and physical absence cause me great and enduring pain but I do — I do — feel his presence and effect on the world when families with sick and/or disabled kids get a smile out of something Henry taught me. He would be happy knowing that, and that makes me happy.

*   *   *

Not long ago, I was acting on a TV show where my character was to witness someone being shot in the throat. The show was an adult action comedy that was a tremendous amount of fun to work on. In many ways, it was a perfect job, because we all got to be funny and serious and scared, and basically run the gamut of emotions. You don't get to do that on every job, and when you do it's pretty great. I knew the day was coming when I'd see someone shot in the throat, and I vaguely thought, 'I wonder how that will go.' When the day arrived, however, I was scared to the point where I could feel I was in danger of shutting down.

With Henry, I had in fact seen blood issue forth from a bullet-shaped hole in the neck of someone I loved very much. Worse than that, I was sometimes the reason the blood was coming out of the hole. At least once a month, we had to exchange Henry's tracheostomy tube for a fresh one, and it could often be a terrible event. It wasn't merely a clinical process; it involved restraining Henry and using both significant strength and fine precision to pull out the tracheostomy's 'cuff', which was a little larger than the hole it had to travel through. And that hole was a stoma, i.e. not a hole he was born with. Thus it was ringed with scar tissue as it endlessly tried to heal. The hole would try to get smaller over the course of the month, and would sometimes bleed during his tube changes. Sometimes it bled a lot. Imagine how you feel when your child skins their knee, and then think about how you'd feel watching no small amount of blood come forth from a hole in the middle of their throat. And you're holding your child down against their will; they can't breathe, they're somewhere beyond terrified and in pain, and you performed the action that made the blood they're choking on come out. And sometimes you're trying to calm other adults in the room, because you're training them to do the same thing so that you can leave your child with them in the event that you want to be able to go to work, or even just to sleep. This isn't an indictment of anyone, by the way. It's just that emergency care of babies and toddlers with complex tracheostomies isn't a skill that most people need to have, even nurses and doctors. And you have to practise on a real kid before you're allowed to be left alone with them outside a hospital. So Leah and I, like many parents before and after us, became very good at all the terrible things one needs to do to keep a kid like Henry alive and safe.

(I'd like to add that if any readers are wondering why we didn't put Henry under for this procedure, it was because his brain-stem issues included central apnoea, where the brain stops sending proper signals to the muscles that control breathing. Each time he went under – and he went under fucking constantly for various procedures – his central apnoea got worse.)

For the reasons above, I found myself feeling fuzzy and slow and afraid of the prospect of watching a world-class special-effects team make blood blast out of a hole in a woman's throat. I asked the director and the show-runner if we could chat privately for a moment.

I said, 'Hey, guys, I am, uh, scared about this upcoming scene. One aspect of Henry's care involved a procedure where blood would come out of a hole the exact circumference of a bullet hole, in his throat.'

'Oh Jesus,' said the extremely kind showrunner. 'I had no idea. Of course, that's awful. What can we do? How can we help?'

'Honestly, I just wanted to tell you so I wasn't alone with this big scary secret. Even telling you, I feel better.'

'Yeah, but is there anything . . .' He thought for a second. 'Should we shoot her in the face?'

'No, no, shoot her in the throat. That will look cool. Shooting people in the throat is cool and fun to watch, and that's what it says in the script. I just needed you guys to know where I'm at, and I genuinely feel better for having told you.'

Looking haunted, they both said, 'Okay . . .'

Maybe an hour later, I dragged the 'dead' woman through a puddle of not less than two gallons of fake blood that had poured out of her throat and chest, and put her in the trunk of a white SUV, next to her yoga mat.

Leah recently walked in on me crying, listening to recordings of Henry babbling, made before his diagnosis and surgery. I'd just stumbled across a recording from years ago. It was his brothers doing Alan Partridge impressions. In the background was Henry, talking to himself in fluent baby. No words, just an accompaniment to whatever serious task he was doing, probably playing with the dishwasher. Fucking music. Oh my God, I want to hear him again.

10

Henry turned two. We hadn't dared assume he'd have a second birthday with the prognosis he'd received. After seven months in Great Ormond Street Hospital and seven months in Whittington, we were desperate to get him home. Fourteen months of weeks and days in hospital. Our basic challenge was that since Henry was a two-year-old with an unsafe airway, he could never be left unattended, even while asleep. This problem had an ostensible solution, through social care provided by our local council. But when kids have unsafe airways, the hospital requires all community carers to have a certain 'band', or level of qualification. If the council can't provide enough carers with enough qualifications, the hospital will not discharge your child. The Whittington was amazing throughout all this, even though they were in fact telling us, 'You cannot take your child home, even though he absolutely no longer requires the level of care we offer here.' Though Henry's unsafe airway remained a massive problem that could fatally endanger him in a second, he was otherwise generally stable. A few months post-chemo, his immune system was a bit stronger, and through physical therapy he had roared into much more robust shape. It was thrilling to see.

But like us, the hospital wanted Henry kept safe, and the council was not equipped to care for Henry in our home.

The reason for this wasn't that we lived in a negligent borough that didn't want its kids to live at home with their parents and siblings. It was because the government has spent years underfunding social care and making the prospect of working in social care wildly unattractive. Everyone uses the NHS, but not everyone uses social care. Thus it's easier to cut its funding without angering a critical mass of people. The insane – INSANE – problem is that creating an environment where Henry couldn't be released from the hospital to live at home wound up costing the government thousands and thousands of pounds more than whatever paltry hourly rate they pay a night home-carer for a kid with a tracheostomy. I even went to my MP's local surgery one weekend morning and explained that I had an idea that could save the government a shitload of money. The idea was to release my son from the hospital. To her massive credit, the Right Honourable Emily Thornberry did indeed contact the council on Henry's behalf.

Leah and I quickly realised how lucky we were to be college-educated white people who were used to getting what we wanted. It's lucky in normal circumstances to be a college-educated white person, but when navigating complex admin and forms and hearings and being told 'No' a lot, you should really endeavour to be white and have a degree or two. We were also very lucky to both be alive and not divorced. I can't imagine being a single parent and trying to wade through all that shit. I *can,* however, imagine hearing my twenty-third 'No' while trying to secure the care to which my child is *legally entitled*, and accepting defeat and resigning myself to purgatory.

The lion's share of this work was done by Leah. I was there for the multidisciplinary team meetings of doctors and nurses, but she's the superior strategist of the two of us and could usually see a few steps ahead of me, able to sense where to press issues, and how to make things happen.

I hope you'll believe me when I say that the time we spent trying to get Henry home safely was absolutely just as stressful as every horrible detail of his medical care. Hours, days, weeks stolen from families who could be playing with their sick or dying child. But instead, they must beg for help in front of roomfuls of people whose government-assassinated budgets have trained them to be adversaries of families with sick kids. And I'll say it again for anyone who missed it above: it's cheaper for the government for a kid to be at home with a carer rather than occupying a hospital bed on a ward. Not that that was our motive, but come on; are you 'conservative' or not?

I am also fully cognisant that if we'd been in America, we would've had to deal with insurance companies on top of all this. Like dealing with the nightmare of your child being very sick isn't bad enough; let's weld a multi-billion-dollar, publicly traded, NON-MEDICAL bureaucracy in between your child and their vital medical care. I daresay it's enough to make you visit your health insurance company's C-suite to 'have a chat'.

However, after many exhausting meetings and hearings that I won't detail further but that radicalised me for several lifetimes, we got Henry home, and the party started.

Having Henry at home was terrifying at first. Leah visited the houses and flats of families caring for disabled kids at home to see how they had set things up. We had to turn his bedroom into a specialised hospital room with some sizeable machines, including an oxygen concentrator, feed pump and assorted monitors. Then the amount of supplies and medicines was comical, and required medium-sized retail-shop-level inventory. The first couple of weeks felt like running a half-marathon, then taking the SATs every day. But we did it. And after the initial fear subsided, we loved it. We were home together, under one roof. We could spend the whole day together, from waking until sleeping, as a family. It felt good and it felt right.

Henry sometimes had to spend a night or two in the hospital if he ran a fever. His immune system was weak and the extra holes in his throat and abdomen, and the Hickman line in his chest, made him more susceptible to infection. Leah and I often remember details that were small for Henry, but would've been the biggest medical calamity in a normal child's life.

Christ, I miss taking care of Henry and doing all his medical stuff. Not long ago, I was walking down a street and saw a London bicycle paramedic pulling up to a guy who had collapsed on the pavement and was bleeding from hitting his head. The man who'd fallen was a big guy who would have been difficult to move, so I stopped and asked the paramedic if he needed a hand with anything. He looked at me suspiciously and said, 'Are you a doctor?' and I mumbled something along the lines of no, I was just kind of used to helping people with medical problems and didn't mind blood. He laughed and said that was cool; he just didn't like it when hero doctors offered him help, because they might be good at whatever their specialty in the hospital is, but he found they didn't often know what to do in common emergencies. Anyway, he said, the guy didn't seem too badly off, so he'd be okay on his own.

He thanked me and I continued on my way, disappointed that I didn't get to help load someone into an ambulance or have an artery blast me with a face full of blood. I missed emergencies and danger. I'd been missing emergencies since the accident that led to my getting sober in 2002, but after Henry I was even worse. When I was in the halfway house after getting out of rehab twenty years ago, one of the kids I lived with cut his wrists, and I took him to the emergency room in Los Angeles. He wound up being okay (physically), but I can remember sitting outside the triage room in a busy, loud Los Angeles ER, and just feeling utterly at peace. It felt like I was at a zen retreat in Big Sur looking out over the ocean and seeing pods of whales, hundreds of feet below, surfacing and spouting mist from their blowholes. Whenever anyone around me gets hurt now, I just get calm and focused and basically envision three lanes they might travel down. In one lane, the smoke clears and they're essentially okay after a wound dressing or a few stitches or whatever. In another lane, limbs are broken, maybe they'll require surgery, and in a few months or years, they'll be back at a perfectly acceptable 95 per cent or so. In the third lane, they have begun the process of falling down a flight of stairs, at the bottom of which is their death. I hope it's not this lane, but it's not my job, in the moment, to know. It's my job to get them the help they need as quickly as possible. After that, I can unwind and acknowledge where they are.

Maybe this will change in the coming years. I know that after the car accident that led me to sobriety in 2002, it took several years before I felt pain normally again. I broke my right arm badly and also my left wrist, and they both required surgery to fix. Afterwards, I could absolutely have taken a rock to the head and, while I would register 'This is bad', I wouldn't suffer or give pause in the way I had before. Luckily, my ability to react like a massive, massive pussy returned, and now if I even hit my head lightly, I whine and swear and get mad at God for a minimum of five uninterrupted minutes for allowing me (me!) to get a booboo.

So maybe one day, I'll panic and get flustered in emergencies again. Time will tell on that one.

In between Henry's birth and his death was, of course, his life. That was my favourite part. Henry led a hell of a life. A house with three boys can seem like a ramshackle zoo on the edge of town: loud, dangerous, and terrifying to the observer. Henry sensed that being the smallest animal in the zoo, he'd have to employ alternative tactics to get noticed. And he did. He was impossibly sweet and calm and lovely, so you were just drawn to him. It was a smart approach, and it worked.

Henry got sick when he was eleven months old, and it didn't take long for him to adjust to his disabilities (he was one, after all, not forty-five like me and whiny and inflexible). Henry smiled all the time. And if he opened his mouth when he was smiling and showed you some teeth, that's when you really knew you had him.

A HEART THAT WORKS

Henry learned to live with his new physical limitations, and the unalloyed beauty of his personality shone
through stronger than ever. He was so fun to be with.
And one- and two-year-olds don't have to be fun to be
with! Some aren't! But Henry was! He was so expres-
sive, even though he couldn't talk.

When he moved home, he exploded even more
furiously into life. It meant seeing him interact with us
in a way he hadn't for so long. Playing with the toys
his brothers played with, lying in our bed with us,
flying around the flat on the little scooter he'd mastered.
He loved going to the park and playing catch with
dogs, communicating beautifully in Makaton, forcing
people to draw him spider after spider, dancing wildly
to Sia and Justin Bieber with his mom, and playing
with his brothers, whom he was crazy about, and who
cared for him so lovingly.

Hilariously, one of Henry's favourite activities was
to thumb through and 'read' a little pocket-sized book
called *Don'ts for Husbands*. I'd bought it for Leah a
couple of years earlier as a (not really) joke gift to help
keep me in line. It was published in 1913, and it holds
up EXTREMELY FUCKING WELL, with such
gems as: 'Don't think that it is no longer necessary to
show your love for your wife as she "ought to know it

by this time". A woman likes to be kissed and caressed and to receive little lover-like attentions from her husband even when she is a grandmother.'

Henry loved to hold the book and flip through it, genuinely enjoying it more than *Goodnight, Moon* or any other kids' books whose illustrations you'd think he'd prefer. If you attempted to take it from him, he would wag an index finger at you with a powerful frown on his face. Back off, Dad, I'm trying to learn how to be a good husband!

During this time, we also began to think about school for Henry. This memory is particularly painful.

We took him to look at Richard Cloudesley, a local school for kids with disabilities. Walking around the school felt like walking around heaven. HENRY? In a SCHOOL? With other kids, learning and having fun? Painting? Doing maths? Getting in trouble? I couldn't imagine anything more wonderful. We had a neighbour who went to Richard Cloudesley, a lovely teenager named Archie who had some of the same carers as Henry. His mom, Sophie, and younger twin sisters were and are wonderful friends to us. Sweet Archie would go on to pass away from his genetic disorder two years after Henry. Our families still lean on each other, and knowing they're just down the street gives me peace.

When talking about the prospect of school with other people, I would say things like: 'We saw a school that Henry could go to.' Never 'the school that Henry will go to'. I didn't want to jinx it. I didn't dare presume it would actually happen, even though his cancer had yet to return. I knew I could revel in present moments as they came, but with everything we'd been through, I also knew I couldn't count on a bright future.

During Henry's last year, we benefited from two amazing charities, Rainbow Trust and Noah's Ark. It was an unsettling journey to go from being someone who gave to charities – or ignored their appeals – to being a beneficiary. Rainbow Trust supports families who have a child with a terminal or life-threatening illness. They pair you with a support worker who spends a few hours with you each week, helping in any way they can. Our support worker was named Fiona – and, boy, was she the best.* She was around my mom's age

---

* I will add here that Fiona is so common a name in England that you could use 'I was with Fiona' as an alibi for almost anything and you would be believed. If you added, 'I was with Fiona down at the King's Head,' you would immediately be acquitted, as this would be impossible to disprove, even if there were multiple eyewitnesses who had seen you commit the crime.

and was basically the human embodiment of the song 'Lean on Me'.

She came a couple of times a week, and she'd just do what she sensed we needed. Sometimes she'd look after Henry so we could leave the house, going for a run or just walking round the block with the other boys. Sometimes she'd do the dishes, and Leah would lie on the floor with Henry, playing games and speaking Makaton. Once, she drove a packed car full of Henry's kit to a cabin so we could have a holiday; her version of moving a mountain to make our lives better. Often, she'd just talk to us, letting us voice our worst fears. We'd tell her how scared we were about losing Henry, how worried we were about the other children, and as we cried, she listened.

She also brought incredible comfort to our parents. I think they felt peace knowing there was someone of their generation who was there simply because they wanted to be, and not because they were a doctor or nurse trying to cure Henry or do anything medical.

Henry loved Fiona, which was most important, and so did we. We stay in touch with her and it is always a joy to see her. In addition to just being a kind person who was attracted to the work of helping families with sick kids, Fiona had a story of her own that was tragic and more than qualified her to help families down a difficult path. Many years before we met, while she was pregnant with her fourth child, her husband Steve had died suddenly. She eventually remarried and her kids are now grown, but she carries with her an understanding of the world and how it can treat people, which families like ours find incredibly helpful. I must confess I now find it difficult to truly and fully relax around people who haven't had some significant tragedy and pain in their lives. Just another one of the many things that make me a fun hang.

Noah's Ark, the other charity that helped us so much, is a children's hospice in north London that wildly, dramatically improved our lives. My heart nearly skips a beat thinking about them, because of how much better they made things for Henry and us. While they have a wonderful physical location where kids and their families can stay if necessary, Henry didn't require it; he received his help from Noah's Ark either in his two hospitals or at home. Our help from Noah's Ark came in the form of trained nurses who offered Leah and me respite, play workers who came and played with Henry, a music therapist, and organised outings for Henry's brothers to spend time with other siblings in the same boat (or ark). Henry was bonkers about a young play worker called Lucinda, and his music therapist, Kirsty, did the equivalent of aiming a firehose of pure joy at Henry, Leah and me. I still watch videos of them making music together on a guitar or a drum full of beans and thrill with love. The happiness I associate with that children's hospice is boundless, and I will be grateful until I die and beyond.

Since Henry's death, I have focused any fundraising I've done on both Rainbow Trust and Noah's Ark. I have not, as some might have suspected I'd do, done any fundraising for paediatric brain cancer. The reason for this is that I saw how far a pound (or a dollar) goes in helping kids who are definitely going to die, and their families – and it is astonishing. An hour with a Fiona or a Lucinda or a Kirsty brings immeasurable peace and joy to a child who is grappling each day with pain, frustration, boredom and fear. It gives solace and bubbling happiness to the parents who are watching their child suffer day in and day out. I'm forty-five as I write this, and so far I haven't seen a better or more instantly effective use of money.

Of course, I don't want any other families to go through what we went through. And of course, if I could push a button that would eliminate paediatric brain cancer, I would. But I cannot. I have been humbled by Henry's sickness and death, and I know damn well that I can't stop kids from dying. But I know who can make a dying kid smile and laugh and feel loved and focused on and cared for. And I like giving them money to do that. I guess I feel that the people who are inspired to raise money to fight cancer are doing a great job at it. And my job, as I see it, is to make sure other dying kids and their families get the same joy that we and Henry got from Rainbow Trust and Noah's Ark. It would be accurate to say that I feel called to do so.

It certainly wasn't just paid professionals who helped us – our family were in and out of our home all the time. Leah and I are lucky that all our parents are alive, and all of them were wonderful throughout Henry's illness, but my dad was the only one of the four who didn't work, and could thus come for the longest stretches of time. He flew from Boston to London many times to help with Henry and the older boys, and was just amazing, logging a remarkable amount of time with Henry, Eugene and Oscar. It was beautiful to see. My dad, along with Leah's mom, Nancy, were the only non–healthcare professionals (other than Leah and me) who were allowed to be alone with Henry. This is because they were trained in emergency tracheostomy tube replacement. My dad practised on Henry on one of his monthly tube changes, and in so doing added the final skill (to an already-full quiver) necessary to be alone with Henry. Lucky him! And lucky Henry. Time alone with either of them is a treat. My dad learned how to do many other things in order to take care of Henry in his unique state, but more important than any of that, he read to him, and carried him on his hip, and took him for walks and rides on the bus, and officiated games and wrestling matches between him and his brothers. Grandpa stuff.

11

As I write today, my dad is at his apartment in Boston recuperating from pneumonia. He had a type of pneumonia known as PCP. Not the fun kind of PCP; rather 'pneumocystis pneumonia', which became widely known as a frequent killer of people with AIDS in the 1980s. Many people host the fungus responsible for PCP, but it's not a problem if you have a healthy immune system. My dad's immune system is weak because he's been treated for leukaemia for the past two years. The reason he may have leukaemia is a fascinating and horrible story.

In 1968, at the age of nineteen, my dad was sent to Vietnam. He and his older brother had joined the Army Reserve in an effort to avoid the draft but then their reserve unit got called up. They couldn't get deferments even though they were taking full college course loads in night school while working full time during the day. Deferments were only for kids going to college while the sun was up, apparently. This was after a childhood where he and his three siblings spent years in orphanages and foster homes, despite the fact that both his parents were alive. His mom wasn't interested in – nor capable of – parenting, but his dad was eventually able to put enough sobriety and money together to get the family under one roof, and from what I can gather, did better and better as the years progressed. In contrast, my mom grew up in relative wealth in a coastal town north of Boston. Her parents met at Camp Pendleton, the marine base in southern California, during the Second World War, before they moved to Beverly, Massachusetts, where my grandfather opened an insurance and real-estate business that did very well. They had five kids, of whom my mom is the second youngest. The contrasting childhoods of my parents, and the fact that they wound up together and had kids, would make a nice Alice Munro story.

Before my mom and dad met, however, my dad was sent to Vietnam for exactly 365 days. If you want to know what that was like for him, he maintains that the films *Full Metal Jacket* and *Catch-22* capture the experience most accurately (including boot camp, thanks to actor and Glock pitchman R. Lee Ermey.) I won't pretend I'm qualified to tell the story of the Vietnam 'conflict', but my dad's recent health experiences have shed some light on a few areas.

Two years ago, he felt weak and tired and had some cuts that wouldn't heal, so he went into the VA.*

For financial reasons, it's terrifying to get sick anywhere in America, but it's least terrifying in Massachusetts, as some of its elected officials actually give half a shit about their citizens' health. You can still be profoundly fucked, even in good old Massachusetts, if you're not a veteran or over sixty-five, and so have to rely on the pyramid/murder scheme that is private health insurance. But luckily for my dad, he's a veteran AND over sixty-five, so he's got the VA and Medicare on his side. The point is, if you're going to get leukaemia in America, my advice is to wait until you're elderly and to have served in the military. If any of the above medical insurance minutiae is confusing to readers, that is because it's designed to be. Private insurance companies work hard to preserve an opacity that

---

* If you're reading this outside the US, 'VA' is shorthand for Department of Veterans Affairs, and it runs hospitals and other services that are free to use for veterans. Depending on where you are in the country, the care can be quite good. If you're in Boston like my dad, it's excellent.

demoralises their users to the extent that they give up trying to access coverage for care, and pay out of pocket or – as in millions of cases – just forego necessary care. If you're reading this and work in private insurance or the American government, fuck off and fuck you, forever. In the words of David Lynch, 'Fix your hearts or die.'

Enough business; let's get back to the funny stuff! My dad was diagnosed with MDS (myelodysplastic syndrome), a blood cancer that can lead to bone-marrow failure and/or turn into acute myeloid leukaemia. This was no surprise to my dad's doctors at the VA when they learned where he was stationed in Vietnam. Apparently a lot of vets stationed in that area got – and still get – MDS and leukaemia due to the US Army's use of Agent Orange. Agent Orange was a herbicide used by the American military to strip the dense jungle canopy so it was easier to locate and kill North Vietnamese soldiers and Viet Cong. Dow Chemical and Monsanto were two of the companies that manufactured Agent Orange. Perhaps you're familiar with some of their other achievements in chemistry.

My dad's duties didn't include using Agent Orange to strip the canopy or destroy crops, but he was still around it plenty. When fifty-five-gallon drums of

Agent Orange were spent, they would take them back to the nearest base. Some of the drums were cut in half and buried a couple of feet in the ground. The soldiers would then use them as latrines. Once they were filled to the brim with piss and shit, someone would pour gasoline over it and light a match. So it wasn't rare to get a lungful of smoke from burning buckets of Agent Orange, piss, shit and gasoline. Among the ingredients in Agent Orange are benzene and dioxide, both of which are deadly. And one of the ways they kill you is by giving you any number of blood cancers. To this day, the soil at some former US military bases contains 350 times the level of dioxide at which the government demands 'action'.

Far, far worse than what the American soldiers experienced is the price the citizens of Vietnam had to pay. The US military sprayed around 20 million gallons of the 'rainbow herbicides' (which included Agent Orange) in and around Vietnam, leading to millions of cases of cancer, cleft palates, mental disabilities, hernias and children born with extra fingers and toes. Something to think about when you hear the government and media clamouring for the next war, since the use of Agent Orange is no aberration, but rather fits in quite snugly with the horrors of modern warfare and the methods used to wage it. Another fun thing to think about is what Creedence Clearwater Revival song blared over the base's tinny loudspeakers as some poor private dropped a match into the godless cauldron of shit, piss, and grade-A carcinogens and felt the *whoomph* of ignition on his face a second later.

Leah and I watched a TV show called *Devs* after Henry died. In it, Nick Offerman's character, Forest, goes mad after his wife and daughter are killed in a car accident. He gets lost in his work (to say the least) and kills people when necessary to achieve his messianic professional goals. We loved the show, and we loved how fucked up and horrible Forest was. While we hadn't chosen the path of trying to reverse time and/or create alternative digital realities in which Henry 'seemed' alive, like Forest had, we looked at his behaviour and thought, 'Hey, buddy, if it works for you!' To put a finer point on it: for us, watching a fictional character go crazy from grief feels like getting into a warm bath.

Horror movies became incredibly important to me, and particularly Leah, when Henry was in the hospital. Early in his hospital days, we went to see *10*

Cloverfield Lane in the cinema, which we quite enjoyed. Throughout the film, you're wondering whether the girl who wakes up in an underground bunker after a car accident is there because her captor is a psycho, OR because, as he professes, an alien chemical attack has made Earth's air unbreathable. Leah and I laughed joyously when we found out BOTH things were true during the film's climax. We were ecstatic! EVERYTHING was shit. Salvation was LESS than impossible, not only for the film's protagonist, but for the whole planet. And just like the film's protagonist, we were terrified as to which malady might kill Henry: cancer, an infection due to a chemo-weakened immune system, or maybe his tracheostomy. You could do worse than *10 Cloverfield Lane* for a pick-me-up while your kid's in hospital.

The film *Midsommar* is modern history's finest example of the horror film as restorative phenomenon. Leah and I had the good fortune to see *Midsommar* in the cinema with our wonderful friend Clara. Clara's daughter Maude died of sepsis at age three, eleven years ago. Her older sister discovered her dead in her cot on the morning of New Year's Day. I never met Maude, but in pictures she has big, beautiful cheeks that I would've kissed a few hundred times a day if she were my daughter. Clara and her husband, Jason, have been incredible friends to us in the wake of Henry's death. They get it. Nobody gets it, but they do. And we are far from the only bereaved parents they've helped over the years.

Naturally, we'd loved Ari Aster's debut film, *Hereditary*, so when we learned a new Aster joint was coming, we got on the horn to another bereaved parent and said, 'It's showtime!' We laughed throughout, and at times I thought I might genuinely pass out. People sitting near us were both nervous and disgusted, but since they were English, they didn't say anything. Mother of Christ, that movie made me happy. If you're mentally well-adjusted and wondering why, don't fret. I know for most people that film induced a state of roiling shock and repulsion. But for us, the film's Scandinavian bacchanal of ritualistic murder depicted a not-unreasonable way to process the grief its protagonist was going through after an unfathomable family tragedy.

Ah, the visceral healing power of prescription-strength art. Hey, Ari Aster, thought you were making a horror film? Ha ha, guess what, asshole? You helped my wife and me survive the death of our son, and be better and kinder to each other and our surviving kids. Joke's on you! You helped us more than *Chicken Soup for the Soul* ever helped anyone. Not so spooky now, are you, Mr Blood and Guts? Hurry up and make us another one, or I'll call A24 and say I saw you rubbing an elderly dog's tummy.

Finding out my dad had cancer produced some very strange feelings in me. Naturally, you don't want to learn that anyone you love is sick. But since my two-year-old son had already died of cancer, I have to imagine it didn't feel like the 'average' experience of learning your dad has cancer. Which is to say I thought, 'Well, fuck. You're seventy-three, I'm a fully grown adult, and you're my father and the grandfather of my children . . . now seems like a fairly reasonable time for you to contract a life-threatening and potentially life-ending illness.' I didn't feel shocked or that I had been robbed or anything. I stress that I felt for him (and me; I don't want my dad to suffer and/or die), but it wasn't a bomb thrown into the middle of my life or anything. I didn't vomit or wonder, 'How will I get through this?' or anything like that. There was an element of numbness that I went in and out of, though I would occasionally get in touch with more standard emotions and cry about it and behave in a way that your average

Joe would upon getting horrible news about their beloved dad. But I was never, ever far from the thought: 'This is what's supposed to happen. What happened to Henry wasn't supposed to happen.'

I wasn't horrified or offended by my dad's cancer, but I was angry that it happened during the pandemic and that I couldn't go and be with him. That felt wrong, and that's where I put my feelings. I wanted to be with him because I love him and didn't want him to go through it alone, but also because I had so recently seen what he'd done for Henry.

After friends learned about my dad's diagnosis, they would make eye contact and ask quietly, 'How's your dad doing?' And I wanted to say, 'He's fucking seventy-three and has cancer, which is a normal thing that happens! What the fuck do you care? Have you forgotten that I held my two-year-old's body after rigor mortis had set in? Did you know I saw it zipped into a black rubber bag and taken from my home by strangers? Why don't you ask me about that, you stupid fucking asshole?' OF COURSE, I love my dad and want people to care about him and ask about him, but maybe they could add a preamble or take out a laminated card that bears some disclaimer saying they agree and understand that it's harder and worse to lose your child to cancer than your dad, who, young and hale as he may seem, is still technically elderly? *Then* they can talk about him.

In the spring of 2021, my dad got a bone-marrow transplant in an effort to cure his cancer. Before a marrow transplant, they really bomb you with chemo to essentially turn off your immune system, so it doesn't try to fight the new marrow, as good a match as it may be. As is usually the case, that made him quite sick as the new marrow began to take over. The first 100 days after a marrow transplant are the most critical, and you have to be wildly careful with the avoidance of germs and anything that might challenge your immune system. Ironically, the pandemic had made everyone a lot better about all that, so while not fun, it was ingrained in my dad and those around him to wear masks and clean things and all that.

One thing that absolutely blew my mind during all this was how my mom responded. My parents got divorced over thirty years ago, when I was a freshman in high school. Why they did so and how they behaved after that is their business, and should they ever decide to collaborate on a book or concept album about it all, you can hear it from them. I'll simply say that for three decades, their relationship post-divorce veered between pretty bad to just about non-existent. It appeared it would continue that way until one of them died.

I called my mom crying one day from London, and told her how much it was fucking me up not to be able to be with Dad and help him. I said I knew they didn't really have contact, but I just really needed to tell my mom that my inability to help my dad, in person, during his hour of need was very fucking painful. I really loved that phone call, because it was the first time since Henry's death that I felt like a child again in the presence of one of my parents. After he died, I had the odd sensation of somehow being older than my parents, or at the very least having seen something that they hadn't, and it had changed me. I felt like no one, even my parents, who raised me, had anything to offer me that could light my path and show me a way forward. It didn't feel like I could lean on anyone in a way that would truly, substantively help me. That was a very sad and lonely feeling, and while it wasn't a correct assessment of my place in the world, it is what it felt like.

That feeling really evaporated when my mom said she would go and see my dad. And she did more than just visit once; she became quite involved in his care in a way that utterly blew my mind, and my sister's. It was an expression of grace from my mom that pretty aggressively reorientated my perspective of people and the world at large. It was a sustained act of kindness on its own, but it also gave me the gift of a parental love that I just couldn't deny. It made me feel like someone's child again; it told me that my mom would essentially take a running leap over a fiery gulf with the knowledge that it would help me.

On day fucking 100 after my dad's bone-marrow transplant, they tested his blood and found leukaemia. This necessitated inpatient chemo, which made him so sick we were sure he would die. I was SHOCKED when he didn't, and instead began to improve again a few months later. Maggie and I were genuinely stumbling around in disbelief. Of course I wanted him to get better, but I found that with Henry's and Tobias's deaths, I had developed the belief that if I love you and you get very sick, it just gets worse and you die. As of this writing, he's managing the leukaemia with outpatient chemo five days a month. Look for *A Heart That Works 2: Are You Fucking Shitting Me?* in bookshops July 2023 for updates on my dad's condition.

12

The lead-ups to the anniversaries of Henry's death and to his birthday are the hardest times. The days themselves are often peaceful because we've worked through so much emotion and memory as they approach. But during the lead-up to the anniversaries, all of us in the house start getting cranky and being short with each other. Tears flow more easily. I find myself in a state of disbelief again. My son died? He got sick and they couldn't cure him and he died? And now he's dead? He was cremated and we had a memorial for him? I talk myself through it so I can almost believe it. I talk to him – out loud – and tell him I miss him and I wish I could still care for him.

It's interesting; whenever I think about Henry, he's always disabled with partial paralysis and a tracheostomy. I really almost never imagine him fully able-bodied or as an older kid who's mostly recovered, which theoretically could've happened. Why?

Unconditional parental love for who he was, as he was?

For a long time after his death, I didn't like to look at pictures of him before his surgery. Henry's left eye was turned in, I'd think. He had a little tube sticking out of his neck and a feeding tube dangling from his belly.

And I missed all the care I had to do for him. One thing that fucked me up badly was losing the callouses that built up on my fingers from operating his suction machine. Human beings unconsciously swallow a litre or more of saliva each day. If you can't do that, you will aspirate your saliva and get pneumonia and die. *Voilà*: the suction machine, which can do a version of swallowing for you. Leah or I or a nurse or a carer (or, after a while, Eugene or Oscar) would get a disposable catheter (not the kind that goes up your urethra) and attach it to the suction machine, which was roughly the size of a small briefcase. Then we'd turn on the suction machine to a very low setting and hold the catheter carefully a few centimetres from its tip. We'd then insert the tip of the catheter into his tracheostomy tube. At that point, we'd use a finger on our other hand to cover a little hole located near the catheter's connection to the machine. Covering this hole would close a circuit, so to speak, and the machine would then suck out any saliva or mucus in Henry's airway. If you've ever smoked a bong, it's quite a similar action. We had to do this many, many times a day. If he was sick or receiving chemo and its accompanying fluids, we could suction him over a hundred times a day, easily.

The pressure created by the machine sucking on my thumb or forefinger that many times gave me callouses. After Henry died, those callouses began to fade away. I hated that. I hated it so much. Please let me have my little hard bumps on my fingers that I can rub and think of him. They reminded me of helping him breathe, which it was my privilege to do. I could touch them and know they were there because of him. They told me that I loved him and he needed me and that he was real.

One of my most cherished memories of the three boys involves feeding Henry after he'd moved home. The most challenging part of the feed was setting the pump that drew his 'food' (beige nutritional liquid) out of the bottle at the correct rate to last for his twelve-hour nightly feed. Eugene, at age six, learned how to do it under our supervision. He was very proud to do so, and Henry was happy to spend the time with him. Sweet, lovely Oscar learned how to do it too! I just beam with pride thinking about them feeding him.

The first time Oscar did it, he asked if he could try a sip of Henry's feed. I said yes, and the boys passed the bottle between them, smelling it. Oscar took a sip, smiling. Then the smile left his face and he threw up on Henry's bedroom carpet. We all laughed joyously, including Henry and Oscar. Oscar has never had the strongest stomach. I remember him destroying the back of a taxi one time when I took the family with me to Ireland to do stand-up.

Watching the other boys immediately transform their home lives around Henry was so beautiful; they acted with all the care you'd want from big brothers. One time, Oscar got into Henry's bed (which was a full bells-and-whistles hospital bed) after setting up his nightly feed. I read to them and Oscar fell asleep before Henry did. Henry was AGLOW looking at his big brother asleep next to him. The greatest possible treat.

I feel bottomless sadness for every member of our family surrounding Henry's death. One thing I worry about with Oscar is that he was the baby in our family for a while, then Henry came along and he wasn't.

Then Henry died and he was the baby again. Then Teddy was born, and once more, Oscar was no longer the baby. Is that confusing for him, somewhere down deep? Additionally, Henry was closest in age to Oscar, so what did it feel like to have your closest little cuddle partner die? I have no training in psychology other than five-ish decades of having a brain, but I wonder about these things. Maybe you can just file it all under 'immeasurably sad', but in quiet moments I do what I think a lot of people do, and try to parse it all and understand it, though that's so rarely possible.

With Eugene, our eldest and our lieutenant and trusted advisor, things are different, and just as sad and mysterious. Eugene is emotionally wise at a nearly preternatural level. In the too-rare moments Leah and I were both home from the hospital, Eugene would ask us to lie on either side of him in our bed and squeeze him as tightly as we could. Thus recharged, he would sense what we both needed and care for us, making us snacks and tidying up. It would be a relief when, like clockwork, he would freak out and cry and scream LIKE THE CHILD THAT HE WAS after his very genuinely helpful (and often quite long) imper-sonation of the adult/nurse/parent/maid that he sensed we needed. In his primary school yearbook recently, for his Special Talent, he wrote: 'I can fix anything.' Sweet boy, I don't want you to feel that you have to.

Eugene understood and he understands, but that doesn't mean he's not angry. There was one night he physically attacked me when we were leaving the hospital to go home to bed. He just needed to rain some blows on me, right then, and I let him, and when he was done, I sat him on my lap and held him. Lately, at age eleven, he's expressed anger at Leah and me, and guilt toward himself, that he and Oscar went to school a few hours after Henry died. I tell him that, after spending a good long while with Henry's body in the early morning hours after he died, he and little Oscar went to their rooms and got dressed for school because they were just good little, *little* boys who did what they felt they were supposed to do at eight o'clock on a Friday morning. They'd spent as much time as they needed to with their brother's body, and just felt pulled along by their normal routine. So I walked them to school and approached their teachers, who could tell they were about to learn that Henry had finally died.

I tell Eugene that if he were the age he is now, he of course wouldn't have gone to school. But when he was six, his inertia pulled him, in what I consider to be a very healthy manner, toward the school and the friends that loved him.

Henry came home in June 2017, and in September he had another MRI to see if any cancer had returned. The big boys didn't have school that day, so we brought Eugene and Oscar along with Henry and his carer Angela when we went in to Great Ormond Street to get the results. I remember walking into the room and thinking it had more people in it than normal. Rather than launch into the results, his main oncologist, Dr Mitchell, asked how Henry was doing. We said he was doing great. Really progressing with physical therapy. Cruising beautifully and crawling quickly upstairs, leading us to believe that walking might not be far off. His Makaton vocabulary was growing quickly, and he was very, very happy to be at home.

'Wow,' said Dr Mitchell. 'Well, I asked because I am sorry to say that the MRI showed that the cancer has started to return.'

Henry played obliviously, beautifully, on the floor. My stomach filled with stones. They told us they felt there were options, like more surgery and radiation, but we could talk more about that after we'd digested the bad news. I don't remember anything else about the meeting. We shuffled out of the room to the area where Angela was waiting with the two big boys. Our eyes met Angela's, and she knew. We all cried. We made it to a little restaurant near the hospital and fed the boys at a table outside.

Leah understood before I did that there could be no more treatment. I am so grateful that she is so smart and so strong. I briefly considered another surgery, and then getting radiation in Manchester, or maybe even a different, 'better' radiation in Florida or Oklahoma. But Henry couldn't fly, and the thirty (at least) rounds of general anaesthesia necessary to administer six weeks of radiation would've killed him, as his central apnoea was growing worse. Another nightmare aspect of paediatric brain cancer is that you or I could (maybe) obey the directions to 'stay still' while being irradiated in an underground MRI tube. A two-year-old cannot, and thus has to be put to sleep, for five days a week, for six weeks of radiation that will, in addition to every-thing else, guarantee some amount of brain damage. We could 'just' do surgery, but the cancer would have almost certainly returned, as it was proving tenacious and this type of cancer loves to kill little boys in particular. So that was it. Leah understood it in her heart and her mind a few hours or maybe a day before I did.

We decided to stop Henry's treatment. We were told we could expect him to live for three to six more months.

One night, soon after, I told one of Henry's night carers, Rachel, that his cancer had returned and that he was going to die. She yelled, 'Oh no! Oh, Henry! Oh, Jesus Christ, no!' She recoiled from the news like I'd hit her. 'No, no, no,' she continued.

'Yes, yes,' I thought. Her response was like water in the desert to me. Rachel was from Nigeria and a mom and a devout Christian. Maybe one or more of those factors explained her response, I don't know. But it beat the hell out of a lot of the English and American responses Leah and I were getting from people when they heard the news. Many people are afraid of you when your child is dying. I preach sympathy in lots of situations, but not this one. Perhaps because my sympathy wouldn't do anything. Life, and death, will kick their own door down soon enough; I don't really know that a lecture from me on how they're a coward would help. So, Rachel, thank you for gasping in pain and sadness when you learned Henry would die. In the years since, I think of it often as the absolute best response I received. It helped me, Rachel.

Yes, scream it from the rooftops. My beautiful baby boy is going to die.

13

We told Eugene and Oscar, who were four and six, that Henry's cancer had come back and that there was nothing more that could be done. They asked if he was going to die. We said yes. We were in our back garden, where the three of them played together. The three boys, whose health and vitality I used to consciously marvel at and be grateful for before Henry got sick.

We told people that Henry's cancer had returned and that he was going to die. Some people you tell because you have to, like our sons' teachers. Some people you tell because you want to, like our friends. Some people you tell because they are a stranger, kind or otherwise, and they've asked you why you are staring into the distance in apparent pain.

We became receptacles for people's varied responses.

There is a gorgeous, wonderful graphic novel by the artist and writer Nicola Streeten called *Billy, Me and You* about her son Billy who died at the age of two after heart surgery for a problem diagnosed only a few days before. Bizarrely, I had bought it for Leah a few months before Henry got sick at the lovely House of Illustration in King's Cross. We both read it and loved it and were struck by the extremely funny section where Streeten assigns a score to people's responses to learning her son died. Clearly, Rachel's response was a ten. A memorable 'one' I remember receiving involved a guy telling me HIS GRANDFATHER HAD ALSO HAD A BRAIN TUMOUR, BUT HE SURVIVED. Are you fucking kidding me? I wouldn't care if your ninety-year-old grandfather got hit by three buses and then fell in a meat grinder! Grandfathers are supposed to get tumours and die! That's their job! What kind of shitty-ass grandfather *isn't* walking around loaded with tumours? Not one I want to meet. Grandparent deaths are like practice deaths, a step above pet deaths, to help you have the barest preparation for a *truly* painful death. And this guy's grandfather didn't even have the decency to die! What a pair of assholes.

A fascinating thing happened on two separate occasions when we told a nurse and a doctor that Henry's cancer had returned and we weren't going to pursue further treatment. They were quiet and comforting when we told them his cancer had returned. Then they cried when we told them we weren't going to do more surgery or radiation. Then they both said they were crying because they were so glad we weren't going to put him through any more treatment. Their relief was palpable, bodily, guttural. They said they wished more parents would do what we were doing. I am so grateful to that pair of witnesses. They helped underline for us that though we were awash with pain, we were making a good decision, based in love for our Henry.

Not everyone was as supportive, and one of Henry's carers, Mira, made it clear she did not agree with our decision to forego further treatment for Henry. She became quiet and withdrawn, and was clearly upset with us. I walked her through the details of why he wouldn't have survived the only treatment option being discussed. The information just didn't register with her. It was very painful, because Mira loved Henry and was particularly great with our older boys – and they all loved her. But she thought we were doing the wrong thing. One thing that Mira and Henry shared is that Mira had a scar on her neck from a tracheostomy some years earlier.

She'd gone into a coma after an accident and required ventilation for long enough that a temporary tracheostomy had been necessary. So she and Henry both understood something that the vast majority of people don't. It really hurt that Mira pulled away, didn't answer texts anymore and didn't come to Henry's memorial. We never heard from her again.

The situation with Mira is one of those ancillary pains that accompany your child's death, like a barnacle on the whale swimming in and out of your guts day and night. Or maybe the grief is a mad king whose dirty robe sweeps up nettles and rocks and shells and stray cutlery and shit and misunderstandings with Miras, and drags them all through your house and tracks them on your bed and your walls and ceilings. You really can't even imagine the compound horrors that build up around the dying and the death itself and threaten to choke you. So much is poisoned. And Mira was a good person! We loved her! I still do! She just couldn't handle a very difficult thing, so she pulled the ripcord and left. We couldn't do that.

Writing about this makes me want to slap anyone who gives Leah or my boys a hard time about anything, even now. I'd like to see them survive a fucking fourth-tier subcategory of the shit they dealt with day in and day out that climaxed with Henry being taken out of the house in a body bag. I don't think Leah and the boys feel that way; they're good, responsible people who want the world to treat them like everyone else. Ultimately, I want that too, but I do fight the urge to tackle people who don't read a biographical pamphlet about my family and then take a short quiz before any interaction.

My favourite historical response to someone hearing about a 'big' death comes from the character Henry Clerval in Mary Shelley's masterwork, *Frankenstein*. When Henry learns that his best friend Victor Frankenstein's young brother William has been murdered, he says, 'I can offer you no consolation, my friend. Your disaster is irreparable. What do you intend to do?'

Perfect. There is no consolation. The disaster is irreparable. I've read *Frankenstein* twice since our Henry died. It is my companion in grief. It should surprise no one who reads it that Mary Shelley was a bereaved mother.

*   *   *

We just didn't want to torture him anymore. We'd seen the effects of what opening a kid's head from the back and scraping around his brain stem did. And if it was effectively guaranteed that, without radiation, the tumour would return and kill him after that anyway, how could we do that to him? How could we condemn him to MORE THAN THIRTY rounds of general anaesthesia? He wouldn't have survived four of them. It would've been more humane to take him up on the roof of the hospital and throw him off. Loving him meant we had to let the cancer spread and kill him.

It was so fucking confusing seeing him bound around so happily, functioning at the highest level of his life, physically and mentally, knowing he was going to die. I felt absolutely insane.

We went to the park all the time. I signed on to do a fourth and final series of *Catastrophe* in the vague future, so I knew I'd make money again at some point. Henry played with his brothers and his little buddies. We'd cry with our friends and family and his carers. We sang and signed 'Incy Wincy Spider' a few times a day. We went to the zoo once a week.

We had a guy who did animal birthday parties come over and bring tarantulas and turtles and weird little mammals. Henry was overjoyed. We suctioned his tracheostomy as needed and changed his dressing daily. We set up his nightly feeds. We took baths and the five of us routinely crowded our tiny shower and laughed and played and splashed. He glowed with joy, and so did we.

Leah and I had wanted to have a fourth child, but didn't think it was a good idea to spread ourselves even more thinly while Henry was sick. When we found out Henry's cancer had returned, Leah went off the pill and she got pregnant instantly. Henry was the first person we told. He knew he was going to be a big brother. What a good big brother he'd have been. He loved to care for little things. We didn't tell anyone else; it was our secret with Henry.

What must it have been like to be pregnant, knowing you would be saying goodbye to one of your other kids soon? I have asked her this question and listened to her answer, but I can't imagine words cover it.

When Teddy was born, a few months after Henry died, he made short work of me by being so fucking cute and wonderful. He's so funny and fat. And he laughs! Holy shit, he laughs so much. I mean, what's so funny?

I'm wild about him, and when I think about him growing in the same womb as Henry, I'm so happy. I had a dream one night that Henry left a message for him in my wife's womb. And it was in a little picture frame, complete with a little nail; Henry nailed it into her uterus. And I couldn't read it – it wasn't for me to read – but I knew that our new baby saw that, and I woke up and it made me feel happy.

Leah recently went on a week-long camping trip. It coincided with Oscar, our nine-year-old, going on a school trip. So it was just me, Eugene and Teddy at home. They're eleven and four now, respectively. It was really fun, because when you spend time with your family in different configurations, you wind up seeing different sides of them. Plus, the three of us absolutely consider peanut-butter-and-jelly sand-wiches to be a proper dinner.

When Leah and Oscar returned, I was naturally happy to see them. But at one point not long after they'd both arrived, I started to cry. I realised it was because my wife and son were returning from a trip away, but another son who'd been away was not returning. If Leah and Oscar were reuniting with us, why wasn't Henry?

I suppose I think we have a rainbow of emotions. I don't know which colour corresponds to which emotion; perhaps blue is sadness, red is passion, and so on. That doesn't so much matter. I still have all the colours in my rainbow after Henry's death. Name an emotion: I can still feel it, and often do. Leah and our boys and I laugh every day. But now there's a band of black in my rainbow, too, which wasn't there before. Or if it was there, I couldn't see it before Henry died.

It's a part of me now. And it should be. Grief colours the happy moments now, the milestones. Holidays are totally fucked. Christmas was damaged for me when my parents got divorced when I was fourteen, and Henry's death just torpedoed it. I could really, truly stand to skip it. I soldier through for the kids, but I suspect they may look back on their childhood one day and realise their father was a closet Scrooge.

I enjoy the ingredients of Christmas: music, gatherings of friends and family, and ham. But put it all together and draw it out for a whole 'season' and I'm out. I don't like being told when to have fun! I like to do it on my own time, organically. If I see an ad that says something like, 'It's so nice to all be together!' I'll think, 'Well, we're not, asshole.' And I know families change shape through birth, marriage and divorce, but ours changed shape because my little boy (who actually enjoyed Christmas) died.

I've also become allergic to adult's birthday celebrations. Now, granted, you have to take what I say about this with a big grain of salt, because Henry died on my birthday. I fully submit myself on this point to anyone's armchair psychological analysis. But I feel like the reason I can't be around adults celebrating their birthdays is because my little boy only got to have two of them. If you've had FUCKING FORTY of them, I think you can relax. I'm so awful. If I'm at work and someone whispers, 'Hey, we're doing cake and ice cream for Chris's birthday at four!' I will go take a shit at 3.57. Fuck Chris; he's older than me and I hate his stupid shirts.

Five months after Henry died, my dad was visiting and his trip was to include his seventieth birthday. I told him we wouldn't be celebrating it. My dad's seventieth birthday! My dad who'd taken such incredible, loving care of Henry. He was cool about it because he knew I was insane at the time, and I'd (hopefully) banked enough non-insane and kind behaviour over the years to get away with it. But I'm now realising I should apologise. Wonder if I'll manage to do it before he reads it here!

14

We had our final Christmas together. My mom and step-dad, my sister Maggie and her daughter, Marie, came to London for it. It doesn't snow as dependably in London as it does in Massachusetts, so my mom brought some fake snowballs made of weighted fabric that were surprisingly fun. We had a 'snowball' fight in our local park that was a blast. Otherwise, we were stunned and sleepwalking through it. It was Maggie and Marie's second Christmas without Tobias and it was our last with Henry. Nothing seemed real, especially since Henry was in staggeringly good shape. He thoroughly enjoyed the holiday season with family in town. For the rest of us, it seemed like we were on some fucked-up island that Homer cut from *The Odyssey*, where things seem normal at first blush, but everything Odysseus touches has a rotten oil on it that lets you know that something is very wrong.

*   *   *

That December, Henry's Makaton heroes, Suzanne and Tracy, visited our home. We'd kept in touch, and I'd told them Henry was going to die. We all signed and sang a bit and then it started to snow. We went out in our back garden and big flakes of snow fell on us. To be with his mommy and daddy and his heroes Singing Hands, in the falling snow, made him very happy. Leah and I were happy too. We were also very, very sad, since we knew this was Henry's last winter.

And so 2018 arrived. Working backwards, I know that it was on the morning of about 9 January that Henry didn't seem to totally wake up. He seemed sluggish and he held his head at an angle, indicating pain. We called the palliative care team at Great Ormond Street, and they came to our house. The doctor confirmed that his sluggishness and discomfort probably meant that the tumour was growing and creating the problems that a large foreign object in a child's head is known to do. She prescribed morphine and gabapentin to help with his pain. The morphine was a bright red powder that I would mix with water, then load into a syringe, which I'd then attach to his feeding tube to administer. I'm glad it was bright red. The thing you put into your dying child to dull his pain should be bright red, like a flag or a flare or a fire truck racing to a disaster. Morphine and gabapentin work, so he would relax, and we would hold him. He got slower each day, as though a dial was being turned down.

A big Lego Duplo ice-cream cone became very important to him, and he liked to hold it in his hand all day.

Rather than wait until he seemed to be in pain, we were told we could give him his medication on a schedule, so there would be little or no pain anymore. I dissolved the bright red powder in water and gave it to him, day and night. I lay with him, and Leah held him and danced with him. His brothers read to him and played with him. My mom came back to London. Leah's mom came to London. They are both named Nancy. They stayed at an Airbnb down the street from us.

Henry began to open his eyes less and less. He held his little ice-cream cone. He was dying. The palliative care team would visit every other day or so. We measured his blood oxygen levels regularly and they remained okay. Nine days into his decline, I measured it and it was absurdly low, like in the sixties (it should be between 95 and 100 per cent). We gave him oxygen and it wouldn't go up. We called the palliative care number and told the receptionist, and she said, 'That's impossible.'

It was one of those absurd moments that surround death that Leah and I have talked about a lot since. Just a sort of knee-jerk functionary response: 'Impossible.' We weren't upset; the person on the other end of the line wasn't anyone we'd dealt with before. We joked that maybe she said, 'It would be IMPOSSIBLE to stay alive if you don't get that number up immediately,' but we only heard the 'impossible' due to a bad connection. Maybe she thought 'impossible' and 'terrible' are synonyms.

His palliative care doctor came by and agreed that Henry would soon die. He was unconscious. I made sure to keep up with the red powder. Our moms took the boys to dinner and some sort of winter light show in a nearby square so we could be with Henry. Sending them out the door was excruciating, as we didn't know if Henry would be alive when they returned. We told our night carer not to come in that night. We lay on either side of Henry on the grey couch that came with our flat when we rented it. We carried Henry out to the back garden so he could be under the stars and in the night air one more time before he died. Leah took a bath with him, and I sat on the floor next to him. He was so beautiful and so smooth and so perfect. His hair was pretty long, as we never cut it once it grew back after chemo. I would've let it grow to the floor and then spun it up into a beautiful beehive on the top of his head.

Our boys returned with their Nancys and Henry was still alive. The Nancys put them to bed and then kissed us and Henry goodbye, and went to their house down the street. Then it was just the five of us in the house. Six, I suppose, since Leah was pregnant. Six people who loved each other and needed each other.

Henry opened his eyes and looked into Leah's eyes around five the next morning.

Then he died.

Our moms did us the incredible kindness of going to the town hall and registering Henry's death. I am grateful for this, as I don't know if I could have registered his death at the same place I'd registered his birth less than three years earlier.

*　　*　　*

My mom and our neighbour attempted to feed Jackie, the boys' bearded dragon. Bearded dragons eat locusts. They were scared, and spilled all the locusts in the big boys' bedroom. They tried to clean them all up, while screaming. I don't know if they managed it. Unlike crickets, locusts don't make noise, so they could still be lurking, multiplying. Henry loved Jackie the lizard, and she's still with us, nearly five years on. Leah carried Jackie on her shoulder for a few hours when she went into labour with Teddy six months later. Jackie calmed her.

I am so happy Henry died at home. I am so happy that he did so in the arms of his beautiful mother, who loved him desperately. I am so happy that he lay between us afterward and we could kiss and hold him and stroke his beautiful long, sandy-blond hair. I am so happy that shortly afterward, his brothers Eugene and Oscar came up and cuddled with him and kissed him and were not afraid, because they had been so intimately involved in his care over the last two years, in the hospitals and then at home. I am endlessly grateful to the carers that helped us in the daytime and watched Henry sleep at night, so that

Leah and I could be reasonably fresh and awake in the daylight hours to parent all three of our beautiful boys. Henry knew happiness and curiosity and love and brotherly squabbles every day that he was home. And that absolutely included his final days. His death was good.

We kept Henry's body at home for most of the day. If you are lucky enough to have a loved one die at home, keep their body there for a while if you can. They were some very precious hours. People who loved him visited. A doctor came by to confirm and record his death.

Oh Christ, he was beautiful in death. In his little pyjamas. We kept the windows open so he could stay cold. I told the loud builders next door that my son was lying dead on our bed and we had to keep the windows open, so please stop work for the day. They did.

The day after Henry died, I punched myself in the face. I don't know why I did it, but I did it hard enough that my nose bled. A hospice worker was at our house, helping our family. She turned to my worried mom and said, 'Oh, yeah, that's normal. Don't worry about that.'

I will not tell you anything else about the moments before or after Henry's death. I can talk about them, but I don't want to try to confine them to ink. Maybe you have experienced something like them, or maybe someday you will.

15

Leah went to Henry's funeral pregnant with Teddy. I don't use the word 'fortitude' often, but it applies to Leah. I love her so much. I need her. I lean on her. I can't do it without her and I don't want to.

Most of our few-and-far-between smiles in the days before and after Henry's memorial service were courtesy of the fact that the very kind and very capable funeral director taking care of Henry was named Barry White.

Lately my perception of time's passing has been noticeably speeding up. I'm forty-five now, which means that statistically I'm more than halfway through my life. My death is probably closer than my birth. Maybe by a lot! Who knows? Not me. I'm in pretty good shape, but things are slowly starting to change. I can't sprint anymore or I will hurt myself. My vision is starting to get worse, and I have to 'take it easy' whenever my kids manage to get me on a trampoline, lest I injure myself. I've had a vasectomy, which means I am unlikely to be a dad to any more babies. I'm not exactly in the sunset of my life, but I have definitely eaten lunch.

Maybe that's why naps are more important to me now than ever. God knows I needed them after Henry died. The fatigue of grief is fucking staggering. For months after Henry died, I really, really wondered if I would wake up whenever I went to sleep. I couldn't imagine that any sort of pilot light remained on once I surrendered to sleep. I felt no animating force within me, no desire or biological initiative or curiosity to see what the future held past the next chunk of sleep. Could my heart just stop, I wondered? Like Henry's did once his tumour grew too large for his beautiful little head and put too much pressure on his brain and switched it off? What thread would pull me back to consciousness after whatever regenerative circadian quota was met? Something always would, but fuck if I know what it was.

When Eugene, our eldest, was born, I was awestruck and overjoyed but I also thought, 'Wow, I am gonna die.' I was ultra-cognisant that I'd fulfilled the big biological imperative I'd been put here for. It would be cool to stick around, but I didn't strictly have to. Seeing him exit Leah's body and watching him draw his first breaths was glorious and awe-inspiring and all that, but watching a life begin made me know, bone-deep, that my life would one day end, conclusively. I mean, we all know that on paper, but once in a while it's driven home in a way that really gets inside us.

Naturally, when Henry died, I knew it a thousand times harder. Not only would I die, but my kids could die, and the order in which it happened was not up to me. I'd tried in the past to engage in some humility here and there, but having your child die is so brutally humbling I struggle to describe it. I imagine God or one of his emissaries beating me with a bicycle chain or a baseball bat, blood spattering the walls and ceiling with each blow. *Sit down, you fuck. You thought you knew what was going on in this world? You thought you had any idea? How dare you? How DARE you think you have anything you can grasp on to for comfort, for security, for understanding? The audacity of your ignorance. Now you know what you can count on: nothing, ever. That you have my permission to count on.*

Why did I need to learn these lessons? Some assholes say, 'Everything happens for a reason.' I agree, in the basest 'physics' sense that 'a thing happens' because something happened before that led to it, but I certainly don't believe that things happen because God had a plan or any nonsense like that. As far as my relationship to any sort of deity, I take a page from Graham Greene's *The End of the Affair*, specifically the last page, where a grieving Maurice Bendrix states after the death of his love, Sarah, 'I hate you, God. I hate you as though you existed.'

With the death of my blue-eyed son Henry, I often found myself driven by the urge to believe in God so I could live to a very old age, then die and meet Him – so I could kick his teeth in. I wanted to be a cockroach. I wanted to survive all the horror and the drudgery and the pain. Didn't even want to do it happily. I just wanted to endure what shouldn't be endured, and crawl on elbows and knees over the finish line and tell God to fuck off. Thoughts like that genuinely made me smile at the time. They still do. They're the sort of dark comfort-food thoughts that bereaved parents share and laugh at.

But I do think it's a good idea to think about death and the fact that you'll die, from time to time. There's also a strong possibility that the downward slope will involve pain, fear and surprise. Most, or all, of your own path to death you won't be able to plan, so I do think it's wise to at least cultivate a resilient, if not necessarily positive, attitude towards it. To be clear, I am purely speaking about our attitudes towards our own deaths; I think it's absolutely reasonable to (literally) rip out your hair and throw bricks through windows when you're grappling with the impending or recent death of someone else. After all, you love them, or you love and miss them. But you?

When you die, you'll be okay.

I have a few reasons I'm not worried about my own death. Here's a big, big one that I'll use the example of birth to help illustrate. Whenever someone tells me they're expecting their first baby and they're nervous, I tell them the following: 'Oh my goodness, that's wonderful. I am so happy for you. Listen, of course you're nervous but here's the deal: you're ready for all the bad stuff. You've been very tired before. You've been in pain before. You've been worried about money before. You've felt like an incapable moron before. So you'll be fine with the difficult parts! You're already a pro. What you're NOT ready for is the wonderful parts. NOTHING can prepare you for how amazing this will be. There is no practice for that. There is no warm-up version. You are about to know joy that will blow your fucking mind apart. Happiness before this? HA HA. Mystery? LOL. Wonder? Fuck off! You are about to see something magical and new that you have no map for! None! This is it. Are you ready for that? Are you? No! No, you're not! Also, please let me babysit when you're finally ready to let someone else hold your beautiful little nugget! First time's free, second time is fifteen pounds an hour.'

This speech is particularly good for dads-to-be, since they're usually more nervous than the moms-to-be. Which makes sense, since they haven't been getting their period for ten-plus years, nor have they been pregnant for forty weeks. Plus, society only legalised men talking about their feelings in 2013.

So while I think that most people who say, 'Everything happens for a reason,' can fuck off to a frigid cave, I am more than willing to extend my feelings around birth on to death, the other big thing we all get to do. We don't know what will happen and it's not our job to know. Just go for the ride, baby! If it weren't cool (literally) everyone wouldn't be doing it. Death is a bridge. And just like a little baby coming into the world brings with it a secret parcel of knowledge you can't get anywhere else, you'll only get to know what's on the other side of that bridge when you're ready (and dead).

Still, I worried about Henry's brothers. I worried his death would fuck them up irreparably. I called my friend Todd, who'd experienced terrible tragedy in his childhood. When he was very young, his dad went into their flooded basement to try and sort things out, and was electrocuted. After some time, his mom remarried and he grew to love his stepfather. He called him Dad. Then his second dad died of cancer. This was all before Todd turned six. Todd happens to be one of the kindest and most sensitive people I've ever known, and is married and a doting dad to two beautiful girls. He's human and surely has problems like anyone, but he is by no stretch of the imagination 'fucked up'. I asked him if he had advice for me in parenting Eugene and Oscar in the wake of Henry's death. He told me that after his second dad died, he and his mom were a little team. They took care of each other and just loved and valued each other, and that, over the years, did the trick. He told me Leah and I didn't have to do anything perfectly; we just had to hold the boys and be near them and follow our hearts, as long as they were telling us to just be present and squeeze them.

Another friend, Pat, was nine when his brother Sean died. Sean was born with a heart defect, spent a year in the hospital, and then died. Pat told me that his parents were shattered. He told me Leah and I were already way ahead of the game in our even wondering how the older boys were doing and how they'd be moving forward. In a testament to Pat's excellence as a human being and friend, he flew out right after Henry's initial surgery and got to know him over a few days, which meant so much to me.

It echoed how Pat took INCREDIBLE care of me after I crashed a car into a Los Angeles Department of Water and Power building while blackout drunk back in 2002. He went to court with me, drove me to surgeries, and in a Lifetime Friendship Hall of Fame move, he single-handedly moved all my stuff out of my apartment and put it in storage while I was in rehab and a halfway house. I couldn't even help, because I'd broken both my arms in the accident. It COULD be argued that Pat got a good return on his investment in me, in that I immediately got sober after the accident and have stayed sober for over twenty years – but did he worry he was wasting his time on an unrepentant piece of shit? Pat, why are you so good? It is with pleasure that I set down in these pages how grateful I am for you in my life.

So the message from Todd and Pat was just to love our boys and be there. Thank goodness that's what we'd been doing. With everything surrounding Henry, the thing I'm most grateful for is that Leah and I knew from the beginning that we couldn't just focus on Henry with tunnel vision. We had to continue to love and parent Eugene and Oscar and – AND! – we had to actively love each other and maintain our marriage.

16

Sometimes in the hospital, I would look at the parents of other very sick kids and think, 'Man, that must be awful. They're in a fucking paediatric cancer ward because their kid is sick and might even die? Their baby? Christ . . .'

They looked so tired and sad, like ghosts. I wanted to do something to help them.

Then I'd remember why I was there. I'd have to remind myself. I still have to.

Our baby boy got sick.

We went to a lot of doctors, trying to find out what was wrong with him.

We found out what it was.

It was very, very bad.

It got worse.

And then he died.

And now he's dead.

* * *

I still have to remind myself.

I will never see Henry again. There is no physical paradise where he's waiting for me, and for that I'm glad. I have to imagine that would get boring after a couple of centuries, for him, for me. For you. Rather, I suspect I am a glass of water, and when I die, the contents of my glass will be poured into the same vast ocean that Henry's glass was poured into, and we will mingle together forever. We won't know who's who. And you'll get poured in there one day, too.

Spider and I sit watching the sky
On a world without sound
We knit a web to catch one tiny fly
For our world without sound
We sleep in the mornings
We dream of a ship that sails away
A thousand miles away.

— 'Spider and I', Brian Eno

Acknowledgements

There are so many people who showed Henry and our family so much kindness during his life and after his death. People who had a massive, indelible effect on his happiness and ours. And many of them are not named in the book! Further, they are too numerous to list here. Friends who visited regularly, some even on a strict schedule. Friends who read to Henry and played with him many, many times. Friends who cooked us countless meals while we bounced between hospital and home. I am sorry I couldn't include them all in the book but I hope my in-person thanks, hugs and kisses have conveyed my gratitude. If you were touched by any of the acts of love and kindness extended to our family in this book, please know you've only seen the tip of a glorious behemoth of an iceberg.

I will single out for thanks my wife, Leah. Not only for all the awe-inspiring things you've learned about her in the book but also for reading early drafts of it and immeasurably improving the final product. Leah is many things and a brilliant, savvy reader is one of them.

My lifelong friend Jon Santer also helped me sharpen the book's scope and gave me the confidence to omit passages that felt like they could have been in any book, but didn't need to be in this necessarily focused one.

I am proud to be able to say that this is my *second* book with my American publisher, Julie Grau. Julie reminds me of the angels in the Talmud leaning over each blade of grass whispering, 'Grow, grow!' Thank you for turning me into an author, Julie.

I must especially loudly thank my editor, Harriet Poland. I had no plans to write a book about Henry until Harriet wrote me a beautiful letter explaining why she thought it might be a good idea. In particular I was moved by Harriet's story of caring for her father, Simon Poland, who died of a brain tumour when she was a child. I believed Harriet would handle this book with the sensitivity and compassion I required, and I was correct. Thus it is accurate to say that Harriet's love for her dad provided the spark for this book to be written.

www.rainbowtrust.org.uk
www.noahsarkhospice.org.uk